Together On A Tightrope

Together On A Tightrope

Dr. Richard Fowler
& Rita Schweitz

A JANET THOMA BOOK

THOMAS NELSON PUBLISHERS
Nashville

Published in Nashville, Tennessee, by Thomas Nelson, Inc., and distributed in Canada by Lawson Falle, Ltd., Cambridge, Ontario.

Scripture quotations are from the NEW KING JAMES VERSION of the Bible. Copyright © 1979, 1980, 1982, Thomas Nelson, Inc., Publishers.

Scripture quotations noted TLB are from THE LIVING BIBLE (Wheaton, IL: Tyndale, 1971) and are used by permission.

Scripture quotations noted NIV are from The Holy Bible: NEW INTERNATIONAL VERSION. Copyright © 1978 by the New York International Bible Society. Used by permission of Zondervan Bible Publishers.

Scripture quotations noted NASB are from THE NEW AMERICAN STANDARD BIBLE, Copyright © 1960, 1962, 1963, 1968, 1971, 1972, 1973, 1975, 1977 by The Lockman Foundation and are used by permission.

Library of Congress Cataloging-in-Publication Data

Fowler, Richard A., 1948–
    Together on a tightrope / Rick Fowler and Rita Schweitz.
      p.   cm.
    Includes bibliographical references.
    ISBN 0-8407-7657-8
    1. Interpersonal relations. 2. Marriage. 3. Life change events—Psychological aspects. 4. Marriage—United States. I. Schweitz, Rita, 1956– . II. Title.
HM132.F68 1991   91-28887
647.7′8—dc20   CIP

Printed in the United States of America
1 2 3 4 5 6 7 — 96 95 94 93 92 91

THE MINIRTH-MEIER CLINIC OFFICES

National Headquarters
MINIRTH-MEIER, CLINIC,
   P.A.
2100 N. Collins Blvd.
Richardson, Texas 75080
(214) 669-1733
1-800-229-3000
OUTPATIENT SERVICES
DAY TREATMENT
   CENTER
HOSPITAL PROGRAMS

MINIRTH-MEIER
   TUNNELL & WILSON
   CLINIC
Centre Creek Office Plaza,
   Suite 200
1812 Centre Creek Drive
Austin, Texas 78754
(512) 339-7511
1-800-444-5751
OUTPATIENT SERVICES
DAY TREATMENT
   CENTER
HOSPITAL PROGRAMS

MINIRTH-MEIER CLINIC
   WEST
260 Newport Center Drive,
   Suite 430
Newport Beach, California
   92660
(714) 760-3112
1-800-877-4673
OUTPATIENT SERVICES
DAY TREATMENT
   CENTER
HOSPITAL PROGRAMS

MINIRTH-MEIER CLINIC,
   P.C.
The Grove, Suite 1510
2100 Manchester Road
Wheaton, Illinois 60187
(708) 653-1717
1-800-848-8872
1-800-545-1819
OUTPATIENT SERVICES
DAY TREATMENT
   CENTER
HOSPITAL PROGRAMS
NATIONAL
   COMMUNICATIONS
   DIVISION

MINIRTH-MEIER-RICE
   CLINIC, P.A.
Koger Center in the Shannon
   Building
10801 Executive Center
   Drive, Suite 305
Little Rock, Arkansas 72211
(501) 225-0576
1-800-488-4769
OUTPATIENT SERVICES
HOSPITAL PROGRAMS

MINIRTH-MEIER BYRD
   CLINIC, P.A.
4300 Fair Lakes Court, Suite
   200
Fairfax, Virginia 22033-4231
(703) 968-3556
1-800-486-HOPE (4673)
OUTPATIENT SERVICES
DAY TREATMENT
   CENTER
HOSPITAL PROGRAMS

For general information about other Minirth-Meier Clinic branch offices, counseling services, educational resources and hospital programs, call toll free 1-800-545-1819.

National Headquarters: (214) 669-1733   1-800-229-3000

CONTENTS

Contents

TOGETHER ON A TIGHTROPE

Part I
Maintaining Good Relationships During Tough Times

1

Balancing Relationships in Times of Crisis

Mike and Patti Carlson were a typical young couple with a schedule full of predictable events. They went to work, played softball with the kids, and looked forward to occasional family vacations. Their children, four-year-old Mandy and nine-year-old Tyler, were happy and well adjusted. Life was running along smoothly until Mike lost his job in a company merger.

Bills piled up as Mike chased down leads from colleagues, the want ads, and the job service. As a father and husband, Mike had always been wise, warm, and fun, but the longer he remained unemployed, the greater the tension on the home front. Things changed. Mike became distant and moody. Patti began to feel abandoned emotionally and often found herself tired and irritable with the children.

The Carlsons were good people having a hard time adjusting to a difficult situation. Like most of us, they were not sure how to maintain balance in their relationships when life kept them off balance. They reached a moment of crisis when they realized something had to be done or the relationships they cherished would crumble under the pressure.

Stress Fractures

Mike and Patti were suffering from what could be called a *stress fracture* in their relationship, a term we've borrowed from the athletic world. Because professional basketball players repeatedly put their bodies through jarring jump shots, lay-ups, and rebounds, they become prone to stress fractures. The constant pounding their legs endure can result in a tiny, almost undetectable crack in the bone. If the bone continues to take the punishment, the pain increases. And if nothing is done to treat the problem, the bone may eventually snap under pressure.

In the same way, the repeated jars and jolts of a difficult trial can eventually create a split in a healthy relationship. The injury might not show up at first, but over a period of time it can become increasingly painful. If these tiny cracks aren't mended and the pressures of life continue to add stress, broken relationships can result. Fractured marriages, families, and friendships are too often the painful outcome of repeated stress.

Stress fractures can occur in our relationships with family members, with friends, with colleagues, or even with God. Do the symptoms sound familiar? If you are currently facing a stressful event, or have within the last year, the relationships you cherish may be at risk.

But a crisis situation need not lead to fractured relationships. Consider this *Webster's New Collegiate* definition of *crisis:*

> **crisis** [Latin, from Greek *krisis*, literally, decision, from *krinein* to decide] 1a: the turning point for better or worse . . . 2: the decisive moment . . . 3a: an unstable or crucial time or state of affairs whose outcome will make a decisive difference for better or worse

Note that things can also change *for the better.* There are ways to handle the strain of adversity so that relationships can actually grow stronger—letting the pressure bond you together, not push you apart.

Have you come to a time in your life when the next steps you take will determine whether your relationships change for better or worse? Perhaps you are at a turning point because of a critical illness, moving to a new community, financial problems, the death of a loved one, or divorce. Whatever the situation, you can now decide to move toward balance and closeness in your interpersonal relationships. Or you can choose to respond to your circumstances in ways that will have an adverse effect on those relationships—generating tension and making matters worse.

Mike and Patti Carlson recognized their need to make some changes. Wisely, they did not wait too long. They took action and came to see Dr. Rick Fowler, a counselor and director of the Minirth-Meier Clinic in Dallas. Later chapters will examine more closely the specific techniques the Carlsons learned and how they were able to bring about positive results from the crisis they faced.

RELATIONSHIPS AT RISK

Not everyone has access to understanding professional counselors. You can, however, learn and apply many of the same principles we teach at the clinic by using the resources within easy reach: faith, family, and friends.

Rita Schweitz, co-author of this book, and her family made use of these resources when they faced a seemingly overwhelming crisis. She and her husband endured stressful circumstances and learned truths and techniques that not only allowed their relationships to survive, but also to thrive. This is their story . . .

In the early days of our relationship, my husband, Arlan, and I enjoyed our times together and didn't really have to work at getting along. When we decided to start a family, I retired as a schoolteacher in order to be home with Erin, our first child. And for eleven months things went well. We were expecting our second child. We had a good marriage, good friends, good health.

Then two weeks before Erin's first birthday, she came down with the flu and didn't recover quickly. She was admitted to the local hospital where our doctor detected a heart murmur. Extensive tests were scheduled at a larger hospital. With each test result we received the report grew worse. Our cardiologist explained, "Erin was born with an extremely rare and serious heart defect which occurs in one in five hundred thousand children. Her blood is dangerously thick. If she hadn't been admitted, she might have died within a month or two from a heart attack or stroke. She will need surgery."

That night we slept on the floor of the pediatric intensive care waiting room. After a medical procedure to lower Erin's blood count to a safe level, she was dismissed the following afternoon. An angiogram and other tests were scheduled for later when Erin was stronger.

We planned to celebrate Erin's first birthday the next day. Instead I woke up with strong contractions, and we dashed to the hospital where Martha was born less than an hour later! At eight pounds, four ounces, she looked healthy and strong, bringing relief that all had gone well. Within days, however, Martha began to suffer from a rare digestive disorder that required extensive hospitalization. She couldn't digest breast milk, cow's milk, goat's milk, or any soy- or milk-based commercial formulas. The specialists had difficulty diagnosing the problem. At first, cystic fibrosis was suspected. During the next few months we lived with the fear that neither of our babies would live out the year.

Martha was put on a routine requiring that she be fed a limited amount of chemically predigested formula every three hours around the clock. She was constantly hungry and upset. Fatigue and stress settled around us like thick fog.

Sometimes we checked out of Children's Hospital with one daughter only to return the next day with the other.

After Erin's angiogram her cardiologist gave us more details: "The trunk of the pulmonary artery does not exist in Erin's heart. No blood reaches her lungs from her heart through normal channels—there is no tube or valve, just a fibrous thread. It's a combination of four defects. . . . She will need major open-heart surgeries to repair them. Perhaps Boston, Los Angeles, Houston, or Rochester."

Surgeries. The weight of the plural hit me full force.

TOGETHER ON A TIGHTROPE OF STRESS

The doctor went on to inform us that the parents of critically ill children often end up divorced due to the extreme emotional, physical, and financial stress, coupled with the lack of quality time for each other. "Fifty percent of the parents in our study divorced within a year of their child's open-heart surgery—regardless of the outcome of the operation," he warned. Then he encouraged us to guard our marriage. Even though we had a strong marriage, his words and statistics were sobering.

As I waited out Erin's recovery from the tests in a stiff recliner beside the iron crib at the hospital, I had time to think and pray. I began keeping a spiritual journal. The more I wrote and cried and considered, the more I realized that I had a specific choice to make. I could choose to let my circumstances control my life, or I could refuse to let them interfere with our love for each other. It felt as if we were walking together on a tightrope of stress, struggling to keep our lives and relationships in balance.

I began to see that my goal was not just avoiding marital tension, being a better parent, handling stress, earning money to cover the bills, or having a family with perfect health and a life without heartache. The goal was love. I wanted to live a life consistent with my love for God, and I wanted to maintain healthy, close, loving relationships with my family and friends *regardless of my circumstances.*

I wanted our faith and our family to be even stronger for having faced these trials together. So I began to read and study, trying to learn the secret of balancing relationships even when our circumstances kept us emotionally off-balance. I began asking: How do you overcome the negative responses to stress—

irritability, depression, worry—that work against the goal of healthy relationships? How do you develop a strong support network while minimizing the strain that problems put on friendships and family relationships? How do people typically respond to crisis situations, and what can I learn from their experience?

PRACTICAL HELP

During this time I became acquainted with the Minirth-Meier Clinic. This medical and counseling center employs a team of psychologists and physicians dedicated to helping families handle their problems. I also had the opportunity to attend a Minirth-Meier seminar where Dr. Rick Fowler spoke on building strong relationships.

I was impressed by Dr. Fowler's insight, sensitivity, and warm sense of humor. I later shared with him my desire to help families like ours learn how to create and to maintain balance in their relationships during life's tough times. Dr. Fowler identified with the need to help ordinary people deal with the extraordinary problems they have encountered, so we began to put together materials that would give practical help to people who felt stranded on the tightrope of stress.

In the following pages you will read about people in troubling circumstances who have done more than just avoid stress fractures, strained relationships, and tension. They have drawn closer as a result of their trials. Their stories are real, and their testimonies are inspiring examples of people who have met life with courage and witnessed the transforming power of love. For purposes of clarity and brevity, some composite stories are used in place of single case studies, illustrating the most common problems Dr. Fowler encounters at the clinic.

CONSIDER YOUR STORY

Stop a moment now to think about your own reaction to tough times. The following list is designed to help you take the first step toward identifying the responses to stressful circumstances that impact your relationships. Some of the statements may make you feel uncomfortable or discouraged. That's OK. An emotional reaction is perfectly healthy. Don't spend too much time on any item, but check the comments that apply to you.

____ *"When I face difficult circumstances, I worry a lot or become depressed."*

____ *"It's hard for me to share my feelings with others."*

____ *"I find myself responding to stress 'just like my parents,' even in areas I want to change."*

____ *"I try to meet everyone's needs and make them happy, even if I wear myself out or make myself miserable in the process."*

____ *"I typically expect the worst."*

____ *"I think my circumstances are to blame for most of the problems in my life."*

____ *"I often focus on the question, 'Why me?' "*

____ *"I feel that asking for help or needing emotional support is a sign of weakness or lack of faith."*

____ *"I'm easily irritated when little things complicate my problems."*

____ *"I feel that most of what happens to me is out of my control."*

____ *"When a crisis occurs, I have an assigned role—I'm labeled the emotional one (or the logical one, the compassionate one, the practical one)."*

____ *"I depend almost entirely on one person for support."*

____ *"I find myself continually preoccupied with my problem."*

____ *"I feel ashamed and guilty about what is happening in my life."*

____ *"I recognize times when tension in a current relationship has been triggered by some unresolved issue in a former relationship."*

____ *"I'm troubled by fears based on a previous bad experience."*

____ *"I feel that God is punishing me or has withdrawn from me."*

____ *"I think it's easier to avoid problems than to face them."*

____ *"I find it hard to admit feelings of anger, resentment, or bitterness toward God."*

____ *"I mentally criticize myself for my response to stress."*

If you checked any of these statements, there is a great deal in this book that can help you. It contains a message of confidence, respect, love, and hope. Although you may not be able to control all of your circumstances, you *can* learn to control your response to them in ways that help determine what impact those circumstances will have on your relationships. You can take steps toward balanced, loving relationships regardless of your present situation. That's our goal.

This is not a book of easy answers and quick fixes. Past conditioning and present choices often sabotage our ability to maintain the loving relationships we desire, even in the best of circumstances. When the pressure is on we may find ourselves behaving in ways that undermine the very relationships we cherish, despite our noble intentions.

A person who is facing a time of crisis and desperately wants to minimize the destructive impact of adverse circumstances on his or her relationships may read the following pages with a characteristic sense of urgency. But we encourage you to take the time to do more than read. Get involved! Grab your notebook and jot down your thoughts, reactions, and goals as you consider your situation. Write in this book itself.

We will help you analyze your situation with some of the tools Rick Fowler uses to counsel people living through tough times. You can learn to recognize problems and restore balance in relationships as you move through the series of interactive exercises, case studies, and checklists built into the book.

The ability of our relationships to remain solid and close hinges on the decisions we make every day. With good choices, good relationships will improve—become deeper, more solid, more creative, more supportive. And even deteriorating or unhealthy relationships can be rebuilt if we are willing to approach the following chapters honestly and openly.

It helps to read as though you will be teaching what you learn to a spouse, a child, or a friend tomorrow, while it is still fresh. This technique brings immediate benefits that will be encouraging.

We will begin by discussing the proper boundaries of trust and intimacy that govern personal sharing when we reach out for support from others.

2

Watch Your Step!

The Intimacy Trap

Alan owned a small family business that was having extreme financial problems. Because he mistakenly equated his self-worth with his wage-earning ability, Alan considered himself a failure. He was hurting inside, and when he went to talk to the bank loan officer he was hoping to find help.

Later Alan reported with disgust, "The first time I went in, the guy asked all sorts of questions about our business, and I told him everything. He seemed really interested and concerned, and it felt good to get it out in the open. Then the next time I went in he only wanted to look at the figures. I thought he cared about us but all he cared about was the money."

Of course the guy at the bank cared about the money

—he was a *loan officer!* He was being paid to care about the money. His job required objectivity. That doesn't necessarily mean he did not care about Alan.

Alan set himself up to have his feelings hurt by seeking intimacy in a professional setting designed to offer factual financial advice. He took the relationship far too personally. Fortunately for Alan the loan officer was a man of integrity, and Alan's personal problems did not end up as coffee shop talk. But they could have.

Everyone going through intense trials will crave support and understanding. Sharing can ease the burden of our problems. But it is not safe to share your deepest thoughts and feelings with just anyone. Such a misjudgment can result in painful rejection, misunderstanding, or betrayal.

Healthy sharing involves communicating your feelings and needs to someone *who is committed to you.* In this chapter we will discuss the guidelines that govern disclosure. But first we look at a perfect example: God Himself when He became man.

THE VALUE OF RESTRAINT

While Christ was on earth physically, He was not intimate with all His disciples equally. Out of the vast crowds who followed Jesus, He trusted seventy men enough to send them out proclaiming the kingdom. He spent the majority of the time teaching only twelve—men He had personally selected.

Of the twelve disciples only James, John, and Peter were permitted with Him in His most revealing moments, such as on the Mount of Transfiguration and in Gethsemane. And only John was given the title "that disciple whom Jesus loved" (John 21:7). Beyond that, there were some things Christ shared with His Heavenly Father alone.

It is clear that Christ did not share Himself or His sorrows equally with all men.

In times of crisis it is natural for us to long desperately for comfort and close relationships. And compassion pulls us to reach out to others in their time of need. But we cannot expect to give or to receive the same type of encouragement in every relationship. Whether we are the one hurting or the one helping, we must let the intimacy and trust level in the relationship govern our openness to others.

Proverbs has much to say about being discreet and wise in what we say and to whom we say it. Consider the wisdom in these verses:

- Discretion will preserve you;
  Understanding will keep you (2:11).
- A fool's mouth is his undoing, and his lips are a snare to his soul (18:7, NIV).
- A man who has friends must himself be friendly,
  But there is a friend who sticks closer than a brother (18:24).
- A gossip betrays a confidence; so avoid a man who talks too much (20:19, NIV).
- Whoever guards his mouth and tongue
  Keeps his soul from troubles (21:23).

Even though these principles seem straightforward, people under pressure often violate them, as Alan did, and end up hurt or angry.

FIVE STAGES OF RELATIONSHIPS

Understanding healthy roles in nurturing relationships begins with understanding a psychological and, we believe, biblical concept called the *Pyramid of Interpersonal Relationships*. Christ Himself, as we read

Pyramid of Interpersonal Relationships

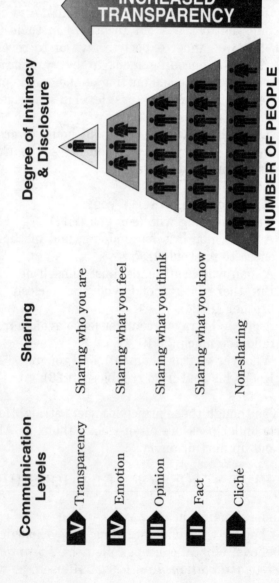

Communication Levels	Sharing	
V Transparency	Sharing who you are	
IV Emotion	Sharing what you feel	
III Opinion	Sharing what you think	
II Fact	Sharing what you know	
I Cliché	Non-sharing	

Degree of Intimacy & Disclosure

INCREASED TRANSPARENCY

NUMBER OF PEOPLE

Cognitive Intensity   Emotional Intensity

90 percent of all relationships, even in church or a close community, are in levels I through III. As the level of trust and commitment increases, so does the level of appropriate sharing.

TIP FOR SUCCESS. To be emotionally healthy, both cognitive and emotional levels *must* balance. Your knowledge of one another should match your emotional involvement. Imbalance will cause dysfunction. When a couple starts dating, for example, and one person gets emotionally involved too quickly (not letting the learning take place) this person can expect to be used or get burned.

At the start of a crisis, if cognitive and emotional levels are not equal in level IV, there may be a tendency for one person to pull away emotionally from the other. This emotional withdrawal will result in imbalance and tension, as will any failure to allow for emotional as well as intellectual sharing. The two people involved must be both truthfully open and emotionally in touch for satisfying closeness and healthy intimacy to occur.

in the Gospels, modeled the kind of disclosure with discretion which is explained below and outlined on the adjacent chart (page 27).

As you read each description, think of one or more friends who are currently in that stage of relationship with you and write their names in the chart on page 36.

Stage I: The Generality Stage

This stage of relationship is our first encounter with someone. At this stage no thread of commonality is required. The setting may tend to advance the relationship to Stage II more quickly (if the initial encounter, for example, is with a new doctor or with a new member at church instead of at the airport or the supermarket).

At this level casual conversation or polite small talk takes place. There may be an exchange of facts: "The bus is late today," or, "The weather is supposed to turn cold again." But questions like "How are you?" are answered on the cliché level: "Fine." People encountering overwhelming problems may, however, be touchier than usual and resent the superficial and impersonal nature of these social exchanges. People who are hurting often want to move too far too fast in the initial stages of a relationship.

How about you? Do you have traits that make you vulnerable to seeking premature closeness in new relationships? Check the statements below that apply to you:

_____ *"I have sometimes found myself wishing that the clerk or receptionist who casually asked, 'How are you today?' or 'How are things going?' really cared about my answer."*

_____ *"I can think of an instance when I was reaching out because I felt lonely or overwhelmed by my problems*

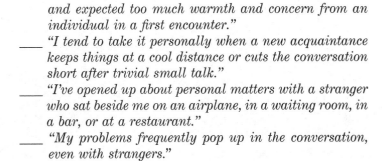

*and expected too much warmth and concern from an
individual in a first encounter."*

___ *"I tend to take it personally when a new acquaintance
keeps things at a cool distance or cuts the conversation
short after trivial small talk."*

___ *"I've opened up about personal matters with a stranger
who sat beside me on an airplane, in a waiting room, in
a bar, or at a restaurant."*

___ *"My problems frequently pop up in the conversation,
even with strangers."*

If you checked any of the above statements, you
show a tendency toward premature or indiscriminate
disclosure. Perhaps you harbor naive expectations that
every person you meet will want to know about and
help solve your problems. Instead, dumping your com-
plaints or concerns on just any listening ear can lower
your self-esteem and frustrate your efforts to make
friends.

Stage II: The Accommodating Stage

Our relationship with an acquaintance reaches this
stage when there exists at least one common bond—
they attend the same church or health club, for instance. But conversation is often superficial or task ori-
ented. Objective discussions hold others at arm's
length. Most of the expendable energy is not directed
toward mutual encouragement, for the word *accommo-
date* generally implies putting up with one another.

We often wear masks in relationships at this level.
This superficiality can allow peer pressure to set relationship guidelines. Stage II generally represents our
public image. This is our basic demeanor when we attempt to put our best foot forward in a work environment or group setting.

Some people sincerely desire close relationships but
seem to get stranded at this stage. Consider Marilyn,

who recently went through a divorce. She wants and needs friendships, but her body language, her depression, and her unwillingness to hold eye contact give the message that she does not want others around.

Jack, on the other hand, hides behind a take charge executive stance that effectively keeps people at a distance. Even though he is lonely, Jack won't let down the image enough to get close to others.

This brings up a personal question: Are you consciously or subconsciously undermining any chance of increased intimacy by getting stranded at this stage in your relationships, like Jack and Marilyn? Check any statements that describe your style of relating:

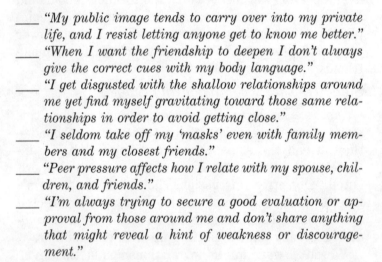

____ *"My public image tends to carry over into my private life, and I resist letting anyone get to know me better."*

____ *"When I want the friendship to deepen I don't always give the correct cues with my body language."*

____ *"I get disgusted with the shallow relationships around me yet find myself gravitating toward those same relationships in order to avoid getting close."*

____ *"I seldom take off my 'masks' even with family members and my closest friends."*

____ *"Peer pressure affects how I relate with my spouse, children, and friends."*

____ *"I'm always trying to secure a good evaluation or approval from those around me and don't share anything that might reveal a hint of weakness or discouragement."*

If you checked any of the above statements, your insecurity or fear of intimacy may be hindering the process of strengthening bonds of friendship and finding healthy closeness. Far from the extreme of indiscriminate disclosure, you tend toward unhealthy isolation. And your style of relating can hamper your ability to develop and maintain the supportive relationships you need in life's tough times.

To counteract the trend toward detachment, think of an acquaintance from a Stage II relationship who could possibly become your supportive and close friend. Having common interests, shared experiences, and compatible personalities will help draw you closer. But before pursuing a closer friendship, we advise you to objectively consider these three factors.

Availability: Is the individual you selected available for a closer relationship? Does he have time to spend with you? Is she interested in deepening the friendship? Does he live close enough, with a schedule compatible enough to make it practical to be close friends?

Maturity: Is she mature enough to handle healthy closeness, or will the relationship end up one-sided and draining? Will a fragile ego, judgmental attitudes, explosive temper, or other character deficiencies inhibit your ability to feel safe in the relationship?

Loyalty: Can the individual be trusted with confidential information? Is he loyal to other friends or fickle and backbiting? Will she stick with you when problems come up and work through any conflicts that may occur?

It is important to choose your friends carefully, especially during life's tough times.

Stage III: The Teamwork Stage

Have you ever wondered why professional football players usually play much better with their teams than they play in the Pro Bowl? The reason is simple: *teamwork*. Some quarterbacks can almost throw to their receivers blindfolded because they know their teammates so well.

In a Stage III or teamwork relationship we achieve mutual satisfaction as more of our external interests and energy begin to gravitate toward the other individual. Generally the bond revolves around a common goal.

Sharing at this stage, however, is generally role-dependent—corporate executives discuss confidential details of a company merger, students talk through academic insecurities with caring professors, mothers share child development concerns. But often that is as far as it goes. Typically, one does not (and is not encouraged to) share personal thoughts or feelings outside the team's goals.

Here's where Alan went wrong. It was appropriate to disclose financial concerns with a loan officer, asking for counsel, but to expect pity or emotional affirmation was out of place. John and Carol had unrealistic expectations that led them into a similar intimacy trap.

When their little boy injured his knee in a bad fall from a playground slide, John and Carol were referred to a pediatric surgeon. They were very impressed and comfortable with the surgeon after their first appointment. The doctor was a personable fatherly type. He spent time checking their little boy's medical history then asked if they had any concerns about the upcoming operation, and he answered their questions. After their son's surgery, however, they felt hurt and misled when the surgeon made his rounds. The doctor, according to Carol, "seemed preoccupied with prescriptions and procedures. I don't think he even noticed we were in the room, except when he muttered, 'Everything looks good.' " The problem? The surgeon wanted to get on with his rounds, and Carol wanted a supportive conversation, maybe even a hug!

Professionals working closely with people in crisis do not seek intimate relationships with their clients because their work requires an objective viewpoint. Your doctor, therapist, or pastor may, however, become a trusted and close friend after guiding you through a difficult time. But beware of one-sided sharing or mis-matched expectations.

Also be careful to keep realistic expectations for those who attend your church. True Christian love per-mits us to bypass the superficial stages of a relation-ship and respond immediately to each other with the characteristics of a Stage III relationship. We can show God's love and concern for others whenever the need arises, as the apostle Paul indicated, "Therefore, as we have opportunity, let us do good to all, especially to those who are of the household of faith" (Gal. 6:10). We cannot, however, expect to be close friends with every-one. Time, both in quality and quantity, is necessary to reach Stage IV. Because of this we are limited in the number of people with whom we are able to develop intimate relationships.

Stage IV: The Significant Others Stage

Each individual is able to incorporate approximately ten to fifteen people at this stage. Here we become vulnerable. We start the process of intimacy by open-ing up and sharing our innermost thoughts. We have a close bond that includes many variables such as likes and dislikes, education, beliefs, values, and shared ex-periences.

We can only handle about fifteen people at this stage because it takes time to nurture these relationships. Ideally, these people include members of our immedi-ate family, our church family, and friends within our community.

Quality time spent together and good communication provide a foundation for a relationship in which we take off our masks. In contrast, poor communication and hectic schedules predictably yield poor Stage IV relationships.

Some people seem to share deep problems and feelings easily, hardly blinking an eyelash. But for others, sharing from such depths is embarrassing and frightening, many times with good reason. Rick's wife attended a Bible study for a while where prayer time was preceded by sharing all types of sensitive information. By the following Sunday most of what had been told in quiet prayer requests was general knowledge among the whole congregation!

Contrast this with the emotional support you receive when you share your heart with a close and trusted friend in strictest confidence. Private information should only be shared with those committed to your well-being in every way. Don't cast your innermost feelings and thoughts before those who will treat them lightly.

Close relationships thrive in an environment of openness and honesty. An advertisement we read recently began, "Nothing binds us one to the other like a promise kept. Nothing divides us like a promise broken." The words are so true. If you desire close, caring friendships that you can rely on when things get tough, keep your word. Always speak the truth in love.

Stage V: The Intimate Stage

We normally relate to one, two, or at most three people at this stage. Often these people are a spouse and one or two best friends with whom we can be open without reservation. Both parties are free to lovingly criticize each other when needed and to praise each other without hesitation.

Within the marriage bond, this closeness often crosses over into sexual intimacy. To guard against the temptation of inappropriate intimacy, it is good for marriage partners to confine themselves to close friends of the same sex outside their union. And those recently widowed must be especially on guard. The energy of the past relationship can be transferred to someone for whom such feelings are inappropriate, such as a pastor or a married friend. In fact, this tendency is so common it even has a name in psychological circles: *transference*.

Communication increases as relationships travel up the path from Stage I to Stage IV. At the lower level of intimacy we interpret what is said by others in terms of our own perceptions and life scripts. By Stage V miscues are minimized because of existing unity of thought and better understanding. And selfishness is often minimized with intimacy; as our lives are intertwined, oneness in thinking and actions emerges.

Be open with those you are closest to. Communicate! But always remember to speak the truth with love, tact, and wise timing. Although our culture emphasizes complete honesty or transparency as the highest virtue in a relationship, do not use the privilege of an intimate relationship as an excuse to impulsively air all your dirty laundry any time you choose. *Saying exactly what you feel whenever you feel it is not intimacy—it's immaturity!* And it will most certainly damage your relationship.

Jean selfishly indulged in bad moods and constantly whined to her husband because she thought she had a right to let him know exactly how she felt. Then she wondered why the romance and intimacy had gone out of their marriage! Love is a more delicate flower than some would have us believe. It can be easily crushed by indiscriminately dumping our emotions. There is a proper time and procedure for sharing sensitive issues. Only our relationship with God can withstand the burden of complete and utter psychological nakedness.

Your Own Pyramid
of Interpersonal Relationships

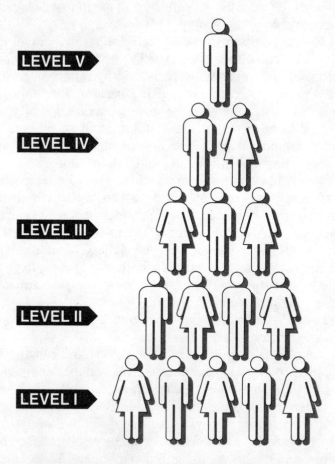

Now it's your turn. Consider the level of
your friendships; then label each figure in
this pyramid with a friend's name.

PRACTICAL IMPLICATIONS

These principles governing intimacy and disclosure can help us create and maintain balance in our relationships during times of crisis. Here are some practical applications for taking a balanced approach.

Maintain sound friendships instead of withdrawing from existing relationships when problems occur. You need the support offered by such relationships more than ever. The corollary also applies: Don't withdraw from or avoid your friends when they encounter various trials, even if you initially feel uncomfortable.

On the other hand, do not share everything about yourself and your problems with everyone. As the saying goes, don't wear your heart on your shirtsleeve. Share intimate prayer requests and problems only in intimate relationships, where there is a corresponding degree of trust and responsibility. This will minimize gossip and unsolicited advice as well as hurt feelings. Alan wouldn't have been offended by the loan officer if he had realized that his need for emotional support should be met through confidential sharing with his minister, family, or trusted friends.

The degree of friendship or intimacy you have with another person does not always remain constant. You may grow quite close to someone who has encountered a similar trial while you go through difficult days then drift apart after the crisis resolves. Or you may move away from your best friend, and find that two years later another has replaced him. This is a natural result of our need for intimacy. The word itself indicates physical closeness.

It may take a week, a month, or even a year or more to grow from one level to another. Open, honest sharing on a deep, personal level cannot be rushed. If at any point you see signs of an unhealthy relationship—over-dependency, any form of verbal or physical abuse, possessiveness, interrogating, dishonesty, or a higher anxiety level when you are together—watch your step! Slow down.

These guidelines make sense, but suppose you do not have a close friend available when you need to talk. Then what? There are times when the very weight of the circumstances will bend the rules. In the waiting area for the cardiac intensive care unit in Rochester, Minnesota, Rita recalls many times when interpersonal protocol was overlooked, including this poignant encounter with a gentleman who appeared to be in his late seventies:

A trim elderly man with silver hair and grey eyes sighed heavily and sat down on the couch beside me. When I asked how he was doing, he hesitated for a moment, then with quiet dignity replied, "My wife's not doing well. She's in a lot of pain. She wants to die. I don't blame her really, not a bit. If she comes out of this, she'll need a heart transplant. Doesn't want to go through it. I want her to fight for more time. . . . It will be so sad here without her. . . ."

And so we talked. The old man's heart was breaking. He needed someone who cared enough to listen. I was the one immediately available. He felt it was safe to open up to me because I had responded with genuine concern and could understand, in part, because my daughter was also recovering from open-heart surgery. We both knew that we would never see each other again after we left the hospital setting, but for those few intimate moments I was his friend. Had it been my daughter who was dying, I sensed the old man would have been there for me.

I didn't know his name, but I grieved with him. A universal understanding of sorrow bonds us to one another at such times. There is a fellowship of suffering that can transcend the guidelines for sharing, a mutual compassion drawing people close in moments of deep despair.

But even if you feel desperately alone and don't have anyone to talk to, there is a Friend who will listen and comfort you. God has promised that He will never leave you: it is always safe to pour out your heart to God. In the next chapter we will discuss how to find safe middle ground when receiving support from others—avoiding both unhealthy independence and over-dependence.

3

Tipping to Either Side

Avoiding the Extremes of Independence or Dependence

Most families make some mistakes in how they handle pressure situations. Strong families go on to make adjustments. A look back at the way Arlan and Rita initially handled the stress of their daughter's medical problems demonstrates these reactions and the lessons they learned in the years that followed. As you read, consider how many of your family's reaction patterns you can see in their story.

Arlan and Rita were emotionally drained when they left Children's Hospital after four days of intense testing to identify Erin's congenital heart defect. They said little during the hour-long drive to their farm sixty miles from Omaha and immediately busied themselves catching up on routine chores when they arrived home.

Early the next morning Martha was born at the local hospital.

After two very difficult weeks, Arlan felt extremely fatigued. He remembers confiding to Rita, "I don't really feel up to handling the AWANA kids at church tonight, but I suppose I should go—they'll be short-staffed if neither of us is there." Helping with the children's Bible club was a routine weekly commitment, and because their church had no pastor at the time, Arlan felt especially responsible. Rita understood the need and reluctantly nodded in agreement without expressing how much she wanted him to stay with her. They made a decision typical of many to follow: They ignored their need to be together and the need for rest and opted instead for fulfilling their responsibilities.

THE RELATIONSHIP WHEEL

When Dr. Fowler is explaining the healthy balance of interdependent relationships, he uses the following model on page 42.

At the top, we see two upright lines indicating our goal: two mature individuals involved in an adult-adult interaction. There is mutual respect and true equality in the relationship. The best interests of the relationship and the other person are considered. True love is demonstrated in action—exhorting, encouraging, uplifting, admonishing, and comforting. The relationship is characterized by freedom exercised in love and by truth spoken in love. This is in contrast to selfish independence or dependence.

If a relationship continues to produce unhealthy attitudes and responses, those involved will experience feelings toward each other that vacillate between alienation/estrangement and an intense, binding need called codependence. This relationship can degenerate into a

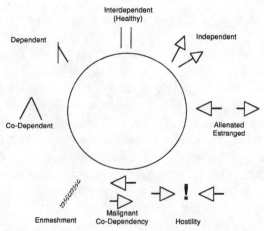

strange combination of total enmeshment in the other person's life or complete, open hostility. People sometimes refer to this as a love/hate relationship with another person.

Finally, the arrows at the bottom of the wheel represent the antithesis of a healthy relationship: malignant codependency. Both persons feel locked into a bitter and destructive pattern of thinking and responding.

UNHEALTHY INDEPENDENCE

Some individuals become overly independent, slipping a little too far from supportive friends or family members during life's tough times. Like Arlan and Rita, who resolved to faithfully carry their own load, these families' predictable response is to work harder, sleep less, and demand more of themselves to manage the crisis. They are slow to get help from others even when the work load becomes overwhelming.

These families generally have many good characteristics; individuals are often known as dependable, stable, capable, committed, and responsible. But they may become the pillars of the community by hardening themselves to their own emotional and physical needs. Often they stuff negative feelings deep inside, believing that it is wrong to feel and express strong emotions of anger, hurt, discouragement, depression, or loneliness. Or realizing that they do not know how to express these feelings in constructive ways, they remain silent. It is simply unacceptable to feel like quitting or running away. They tend to deny or discount the degree to which they are emotionally affected by the crisis—on the outside they continue to appear composed and thinking clearly.

People accustomed to leadership roles in their church or community may feel pressured to manage things well. And strong, giving, caring individuals may have difficulty learning to receive. Here are three helpful guidelines for those of us who tend toward hyperindependence.

1. Make Your Needs Known

In the months that followed the birth of Rita and Arlan's second child, Martha, both husband and wife took turns with the feeding, seldom getting longer than two-and-a-half hours of uninterrupted sleep.

Because the hospital was out of town, Arlan and Rita split the responsibility for staying with Martha whenever she was admitted. They developed a tag team style, splitting up so that one could cover the duties at home and care for Erin while the other remained with Martha. Often Rita stayed with Martha several days before Arlan could come to take over. On one visit Rita fought back the tears when Arlan said, "Erin learned to walk this past week while you were gone."

Rita and Arlan did a good job of keeping friends updated on the girls' health, but they were slow to let anyone know *specifically* what they could do to help. Had they known, friends would have willingly eased the times of separation by taking Erin to Omaha to be with Rita more often. Or they could have taken over the morning farm chores once in a while so that Arlan could make the drive to be with the family. But because Arlan and Rita were reluctant to impose upon their friends, they tipped toward isolation.

After one long stretch of days spent beside the crib in Martha's hospital room, Rita looked forward to Arlan coming to take her place. "When Arlan arrived that morning I left for home after just a short conversation. I was so exhausted I could barely drive," Rita remembers. "When I got home I went to where Erin was staying, played with her for an hour or so, then went home to take a nap. With a great sense of relief I climbed into bed—and woke up nearly twenty-four hours later! I was surprised at the time that had passed, and quickly ate, cleaned up, and rushed over to see Erin again before returning to the hospital."

Looking back, Arlan and Rita agree that Martha required constant care at this time. But they can see that it was dangerous to push themselves to that extreme. Their sleep deprivation coupled with the stress could have resulted in emotional or physical collapse, or an accident while driving or operating farm equipment. Had they been more willing to make their needs known, their friends could have stayed with Martha occasionally to allow them some uninterrupted sleep. As the years passed, Arlan and Rita learned to be more specific when letting close friends know how they could help.

Arlan and Rita also denied their needs for companionship and closeness within their marriage. The commitment to be there for their children crowded out their time together. They took their strong marriage for granted.

Having an overdeveloped sense of responsibility is

only one of many reasons people fail to share their needs or families become independent units, resolved to handle things on their own. Because Mike Carlson felt that others would not or could not help, he refused to talk about his struggle with unemployment—even with his wife and close friends. "I can see now that I've hurt Patti and the kids a lot by withdrawing and refusing to talk. It's one thing to cut myself off from prying people who don't care about me but are only interested in the latest gossip. But it's another thing to shut out the loved ones I've promised to share my life with."

Mike had to work at being close and opening up to his wife and children. His natural instinct when he was threatened by a major problem was to clam up and to assume (incorrectly) that no one would really understand or that talking wouldn't do any good because the circumstances would not change. This false belief nearly cost him his marriage. Fortunately he learned to give up the destructive habit of silence and the false safety of always keeping his own company.

For some individuals the independent, loner style of response is a means of emotional escape, a way to withdraw from the scene of strong emotions and keep a safe distance from pain and uncertainty. This self-imposed emotional detachment offers false protection at the expense of wounding others and weakening relationships.

Refusing to communicate with family members is felt as rejection and emotional abandonment. The person walled out by deliberate silence receives the unspoken message loud and clear: You are not important enough for me to talk to you or share my life with you. I don't trust you enough to share intimately. And your feelings don't matter enough for me to listen or take time to talk. I choose not to be close to you.

Prolonged silence and hyperindependence is selfish. Not only is poor communication harmful to relationships, but also it fosters poor problem solving. As one man put it, "Anything mentionable is manageable."

How about you? Take a moment to look honestly at your habitual response to tough times. Check any statements that apply to you personally, then consider your family as a unit.

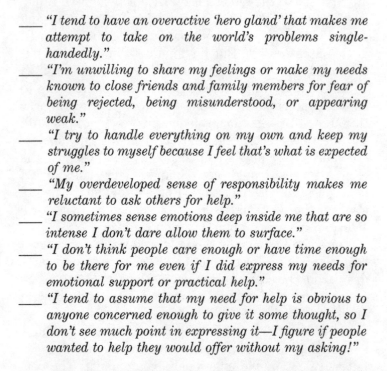

____ *"I tend to have an overactive 'hero gland' that makes me attempt to take on the world's problems single-handedly."*

____ *"I'm unwilling to share my feelings or make my needs known to close friends and family members for fear of being rejected, being misunderstood, or appearing weak."*

____ *"I try to handle everything on my own and keep my struggles to myself because I feel that's what is expected of me."*

____ *"My overdeveloped sense of responsibility makes me reluctant to ask others for help."*

____ *"I sometimes sense emotions deep inside me that are so intense I don't dare allow them to surface."*

____ *"I don't think people care enough or have time enough to be there for me even if I did express my needs for emotional support or practical help."*

____ *"I tend to assume that my need for help is obvious to anyone concerned enough to give it some thought, so I don't see much point in expressing it—I figure if people wanted to help they would offer without my asking!"*

If any of the above responses are true of you, you are leaning toward unhealthy self-sufficiency and emotional detachment. Try to be your own counselor. If you are unwilling to lean on others even during times of severe hardship, ask yourself why. And teach yourself to recognize when it is wise to let others help. Work toward a balance between self-reliance and seeking support.

2. Learn When to Let Others Help

"While I cleaned the house and Arlan was out doing chores, I often felt emotionally drained and lonely," Rita recalls. "But the work was necessary. And it appeared that Arlan and I had no choice but to be work addicts. We couldn't afford to hire domestic or farm help, and Arlan had to work long hours to cover our mounting medical expenses. So whenever I felt overwhelmed I brought myself up short with thoughts like, *If you don't do it, it won't get done. Just do the next thing—and try to do it more cheerfully!*"

During these difficult months Arlan, a former collegiate weight lifter, dropped from a muscular 200 pounds to 174—less than he had weighed in high school. And Rita quickly lost the weight gained during pregnancy and then some. Although they continued to push themselves to keep up with routine responsibilities along with the medical problems, they were literally wearing themselves too thin.

Of course there is value in proper self-discipline and the willingness to work hard. Wallowing in self-pity will not improve difficult circumstances. But it is much more difficult to maintain a pleasant disposition and close relationships when you are exhausted. If you are losing your health to gain control over your life, it is past time to learn when to let others help.

Rita reports that she and Arlan are growing a little smarter in this respect. "Now when we anticipate a stressful event, our first reflex question is, 'What can we drop or delegate, and what must simply be left undone for now?' We're learning the value of stripping down our schedule, delegating what we can and asking for help as needed on the remaining tasks."

How about you? Do you tell yourself, "I can manage my problems without help [often termed *interference*] from others?" If so, you need to humbly admit your need for support. If you fall overboard into a sea of troubles, don't just start swimming across the ocean for shore—call for help! Learn to let friends throw out the life preserver and pull you to safety.

3. Give Yourself Permission to Have Limits

At the hospital Arlan and Rita were confronted not only with the medical problems their babies faced, but also with those of numerous other children whose cries they heard constantly. At one point there were eleven leukemia patients on the same floor as Martha.

One of those patients was Amber, a lonely little girl who looked to be around six years old. Rita taught her how to make paper hats and other craft projects while Martha slept. During the day Amber would push Martha around and around the halls in a stroller to comfort her while Rita walked along behind pushing their I.V. poles. Amber was sad to see Martha check out of the hospital. And when Martha was readmitted about two weeks later, Rita immediately stopped by Amber's room to say hello. The room was empty. The nurse said Amber's bone marrow transplant had been unsuccessful.

At that point Rita gave herself permission to have an emotional limit for the first time during the ordeal. She called a friend and confided, "I can't take any more of this right now. I've got to get away from the hospital for a while." In the same way, everyone who is going through a stressful situation needs to give themselves permission to take a break now and then. Understanding friends can facilitate temporary breaks and times of refreshment, even if it is simply leaving the hospital for a brisk walk.

People under intense pressure sometimes need to be reminded that it is OK to be human—to have ordinary limits on how long they can go without sleep, how much new information they can take in during a single hour, how much abrupt change they can tolerate.

This *superman* or *superwoman* sentiment is prevalent in our society, stressing independence and individualism. Philosophical thought that maintains man is the master of his own destiny also insists: *Whatever the mind can conceive I can achieve,* and *There is no limit to what we can accomplish with positive thinking and persistence.* The problem is that we are not encouraged to recognize our need for one another.

"God will never give you more than you can handle," we are sometimes told. But we are seldom reminded that God does not expect us to make it on our own. We were created to need God and to need one another. All humans have emotional, physical, and mental limits that cannot be ignored in healthy relationships. Distorted thinking makes us feel guilty or ashamed for admitting, "God, I can't handle this alone."

Patti Carlson could not give herself permission to verbally express her inner pain and discouragement to her husband. But her body told him. Through fatigue, headaches, backaches, colds, flu, and extreme menstrual cramps, Patti's body reacted to the hurt bottled inside her. Physical illness was, by default, the language used to cry out, "Please pay attention to me. I don't feel good; I need to be cared for."

Are you like Patti, unwilling or unable to accept and express legitimate needs? Do you ever slip into the superman syndrome, holding yourself to unrealistic expectations and schedules? The following checklist will indicate if this is an area of concern in your life. Check the statements that are true of you.

____ *"It's difficult for me to accept limits on how much I can do or how much I can help."*

_____ *"When I overextend myself, I tend to deny or minimize the negative impact my fatigue, irritability, or moodiness has on my relationships."*

_____ *"I know that most people need eight to ten hours of sleep a night, but I can get by on less."*

_____ *"It doesn't really bother me to skip meals or work through noon hours and breaks when I have a deadline."*

_____ *"I can't remember the last time I told someone I needed them or couldn't make it without their help."*

No one is invincible. Healthy relationships make a point to operate within the comfort zone of normal limits and not push people to extremes. As one woman joked, "My mom always got up early and stayed up late doing things for Dad. We kids didn't think it was such a smart idea. It was great for Dad, and Mom meant well —but when you get that tired someone's going to suffer!"

If you have a tendency to push yourself to the limit doing your duty, or if you tip toward the independent and detached side of the relationship wheel, be sure that you make an effort to open yourself to supportive friends. No one is harder to help than a friend who insists he doesn't need any!

We all like to be thought of as independent, self-sufficient, take-care-of-ourselves people, but too much of a good thing is not a good thing. Once you become aware of an imbalanced response, you can make adjustments to compensate for negative tendencies, just as the Schweitz family did.

Arlan and Rita accepted more help from friends and family during Erin's most recent open-heart surgery. In contrast to spending most of the time in Omaha alone, they contacted a pastor in Rochester, Minnesota who was kind enough to visit Erin's hospital room every few days. Rita's cousin, a doctor at the Mayo Clinic, also stopped by.

Their local pastor and his wife brought Martha up for a visit the day after the operation. And close friends Pam and Randy Cates made the trip a few days later to bring Martha again, allowing Arlan and Rita a respite from the hospital for the evening. Grandma Garton took care of Arlan and Rita's two little boys, Cale and Evan. And Grandma and Grandpa Schweitz looked after things on the farm. Other friends mowed the grass, brought food, phoned regularly, and prayed for them.

This support network made the stressful event much easier on the entire family. In the same way, your family will benefit from staying connected to loved ones and accepting their help and companionship during hard times. Don't try to go it alone. But watch out for the tendency to over-correct by sliding to the opposite extreme.

AVOIDING UNHEALTHY DEPENDENCE

Once upon a time there was a little boy named David who lived in the land of *you*—*you* take care of me; *you* meet my needs; *you* are responsible for my survival and happiness. If things don't work out well, *you* are to blame for the results; *you* didn't come through for me. David was dependent.

During his teen years David wandered into the confusing and lonely wilderness of *I*—*I* can do it myself. *I* can make my own decisions. *I* am self-reliant and solely responsible for my own life. *I* no longer need you. David was independent.

Happily, David ended up in the land of adulthood, commonly known as the land of *we*—*we* can do it together; *we* can love one another; *we* can cooperate. I consider your best interests as well as my own so that *we* will both benefit. *We* freely choose to bond in love and to support one another. I can choose to sacrificially serve you; I can give of myself to encourage your obedience to the God to whom *we* are accountable. David was interdependent.

This parable of the process of coming into mature adulthood will be discussed later in this chapter to help us distinguish between healthy and unhealthy relationships. Dependency gives off a lot of mixed signals. Dependent people need others to do things for them. Sometimes that's appropriate; at other times that's dysfunctional. And people are often confused when they try to discern the difference. Misuse and misunderstanding of terms such as *codependency* and *caregiving* have distorted the perception of how love ought to function.

For the purpose of illustration, imagine a woman named Debbie who was close friends with her sixty-year-old neighbor, Mardelle. When Mardelle slipped on a rug, breaking her ankle and bruising her elbow in the fall, Debbie and others in the neighborhood were quick to offer help. Mardelle was *physically dependent* for a time because of her injuries, but that posed no threat to the health of their friendship.

But suppose that as the days passed, there was a subtle shift in their relationship. Mardelle enjoyed the extra attention. And Debbie liked feeling needed and did not mind the inconvenience of numerous demands —at first. Although Mardelle's health steadily improved, she became less willing to do the things she was capable of doing and reluctant to resume her old responsibilities.

Do you see how easily their friendship could start to slip to the dependent side of the relationship wheel? What problems would arise if Debbie became *emotionally dependent*—basing her sense of worth and identity on her role as caregiver? How will the relationship be damaged if Mardelle becomes *intellectually dependent* —counting on Debbie to do her thinking for her and to solve the problems of her life?

Think back to David's journey through the land of dependency. There are some common indications that a relationship has tipped to the dependent side where someone else is responsible to meet my needs and others are to blame for my problems. One person may begin to feel trapped, manipulated, or unfairly blamed. Control in the relationship often becomes one-sided, with individuals assuming a parent-child rather than adult-adult role. For instance, in a cult people are dependent upon the leader to think for them and determine their opinions. Improper authority is given to one person in the relationship.

In Debbie's case she could begin to resent the increasing demands on her time and yet feel guilty and selfish for feeling that way. In an ideal situation Debbie would wisely decide to talk to Mardelle and to set some limits instead of simply withdrawing or letting resentment build. Debbie would encourage what was truly best for Mardelle: that she begin to resume a normal routine as soon as possible. And Debbie would also reassure Mardelle that she was willing to help out when it was really necessary and would continue to spend time with her even after her ankle was healed. In a happy ending, of course, both women grow to love and appreciate each other more after handling the crisis well together.

HOW ABOUT YOU?

Those who have become overly dependent may cling like a static-filled sweater to the person who gives the love and support they desperately seek. The dependent person may monopolize the supportive person's time and be possessive and jealous of time spent with others. When the demands on the other individual's time become so great that attempts are made to cut back, the dependent person may experience the action as rejection and abandonment.

Try to identify times in your own relationships when this behavior pattern has surfaced. Can you think of instances when the random search-and-cling tendency of those in crisis has influenced your own responses? Have you monopolized a friend's time or placed unrealistic demands on other family members? Have you been slow to reassume your normal load after the initial crisis has passed? Or have you rushed to the rescue, taking a parent-child role with another adult and enabling them to remain dysfunctionally dependent on you? Although there is security and comfort in being taken care of, prolonged dependency behaviors will harm your relationships—whether you are giving or receiving the support.

If you are currently going through tough times, look closely at your attachment to your physician, counselor, minister, and supportive friends. Are you receiving nearly all of your emotional support from one person? If so, it may signal that you are becoming overly dependent in that relationship. Are you expecting others to make decisions or take over responsibilities you could manage? Beware of taking a passive, victim role in your relationships. Watch for signs of imbalance.

Rather than depending heavily on one close friend, picture yourself an active part of a support team that includes many friends and family members. In the next chapter we will talk more about the team effort and how to make it work.

4

Don't Look Down

Seeing and Facing What Is

Dr. Fowler remembers the first time he met with Mike and Patti Carlson:

Mike, a dark-haired man with a tall athletic frame, shuffled into my office. His feet brushed back the fringes of the Oriental rug as he settled into the corner of the couch. His wife, Patti, a trim brunette with delicate features, came in quietly behind him and sat in the armchair. When I began by asking some general questions, Mike and Patti answered politely in turn, their bodies shifting slightly away from each other as they described the change in their relationship after Mike was laid off.

About fifteen minutes into our first session, Mike expressed concern that his lack of confidence was preventing him from pursuing the opportunities for employment that stretched beyond his past experience. I asked whether he, as a child, had been encouraged to explore new territory. Mike straightened up on the couch and began to answer, talking noticeably louder and faster than before:

"You wouldn't believe how protective my mother was. She was always nagging at me not to do this or that because I might get hurt. You know, the 'don't try that, you're not old enough,' 'don't go there, it's not safe,' 'don't forget to drive carefully' routine. Even after I weighed more than 200 pounds, she still harped, 'don't lift that, it might be too heavy for you' every time I unloaded furniture coming home from college!"

Further questions revealed that Mike's mother had been quite controlling and personally insecure. She viewed every choice Mike made as an all-or-nothing commitment. There was no room to make a mistake, let alone change your mind, without being pronounced a failure. Meanwhile, Mike's father had taken a passive role.

The trigger event, such as losing a job, may not be the only problem or even the most important one a family faces. In this chapter we ask and help you answer three very basic questions: What really is the problem? Who's on my team? When is it important to ask why this is happening to me?

WHAT IS THE PROBLEM?

As is often the case, Mike's current response to the financial crisis at hand was influenced by past conditioning. The inner tape of his mother's nagging was overriding the more recent decade of success in the work force. His confidence was leaking out through holes pricked in the fabric of his self-image years earlier. Getting past the fear that a new job would overtax his capacities was an essential step in surmounting these stressful times.

When Dr. Fowler asked Patti how she felt Mike's past had affected their relationship, she shrugged and said, "Mike sometimes gives up on himself too quickly. He has a lot of ability and could be good at just about anything he wants to be good at. I used to encourage him to try new things. But . . . well . . . um . . . he doesn't take advice from females too well!" She giggled nervously and looked at Mike. When he grinned, she grinned.

Often a constellation of problems surface when a trigger event upsets a relationship. The confidence or insecurity of both individuals, prior communication patterns, and the impact of past conditioning and experiences are common causes of discord. In fact, Dr. Fowler has noticed that in over half the cases he sees, the original problem causing a couple to seek help is not the major cause of stress in their lives. *Quite often a crisis not only creates new problems, but also it exposes old ones.*

For example, if we as children were loved for our achievements and our performance rather than unconditionally accepted, we may feel anxiety, self-doubt, or even worthlessness when our achievements or performance are threatened. The problem then becomes one of perceived loss of identity or selfhood, not just the external loss of money, health, or a job. And our emotional reaction and physiological arousal will be disproportionate to the trigger event. A parent, a career, or even a memory can exert hidden power over relationships.

Are there any ghosts from the past haunting your

crisis situation? Look for the faint trace of a previously unresolved conflict, past conditioning, or powerful memories that may be influencing your relationships now. Write down any fears, past experiences, desires for parental approval, or anything you feel still exerts an influence. Then discuss these issues together.

Here's an example of something that needed to be brought out in the open: When Arlan and Rita found out the situation with their infants was life-threatening, they immediately sensed how strongly the past was influencing their responses. Because Rita's father had been killed instantly in an automobile accident when she was twelve, the thought of abrupt and untimely death was tied to vivid and painful memories. It was a reality that could strike again. For Arlan, who had no experience with the death of a close family member except the peaceful passing of those in their eighties or nineties, the possibility of death was upsetting but seemed remote and unlikely. The different intensities of their emotional responses to the doctor's report could have caused friction if they had not realized that their reactions resulted from contrasting past experiences.

Learning to cope with problems through denial is a common survival mechanism that can also create new problems and disrupt relationships. If family members deny what is going on in the face of a difficult situation, or deny the hurt of what is happening, then relationships will be strained. When individuals refuse to acknowledge impact of the events on their lives, communication becomes superficial or phony. We have all heard the old remedy for fear of heights—just don't look down! But we cannot simply close our eyes and walk across the tightrope of stress. The difficulties do not go away when we ignore them.

Arlan and Rita were surprised to find that many

people responded to Erin's heart problem not by offering understanding and comfort, but by ignoring or denying the condition. Common remarks were, "But she looks so good and got along fine for the first few months. Surely it isn't as serious as they say." And, "Maybe she'll just outgrow it." It was often necessary to explain that just as babies born without a hand do not grow one later, infants born without the trunk of the pulmonary artery do not outgrow the problem.

Denying our problems will only create misunderstanding and distance in relationships. We must be willing to commit ourselves to reality, even if it brings pain. When we fantasize that things are different than they are or cling to the make-believe and idealistic world of our daydreams, we abandon our family. Hiding behind ignorance or denial may be a means to temporarily avoid the pain, but it comes at high cost to the relationships we cherish.

Take a moment now to identify the central and peripheral problems influencing one of your relationships. Ask yourself if you are denying or ignoring a major cause of stress. Be honest. Once the contributing stressors are identified, you are free to work together to handle them. On one page in your journal make two lists, a list of big problems affecting your relationship and a list of smaller problems that also require your attention. At the same time, have the other person write out the same two lists without discussing them with you.

After you separately complete the lists, compare your perspective of the problem issues with those of your spouse or friend. Explain your placement of the items to each other, keeping in mind that there is no right way to do the exercise. What can you gather from the lists? Do you agree on the major stressors? Do you see different facets of the problem in the same proportion, or are some big problems on your list not even mentioned by the other person?

WHO'S ON YOUR TEAM?

A good starting point for restoring balance in any relationship is to make the commitment to unite against the problems you have identified rather than turning against each other. That is not always easy—when we are irritated and frustrated by a major problem, we often become irritated with those around us. We may fight each other instead of attacking the problem. It is especially hard to unite to work on the situation if there are any past resentments and tensions in the relationship.

When we are under extreme pressure it is natural to want God or our spouse or our friends or *someone* to do something to ease the strain. If that doesn't occur on our timetable, we may shift our attention from confronting the problem to confronting the people. When we are hurting it is easy to get caught up in criticizing others. But it is essential for the couple, or the family, to be on the same team. As Jesus said, a "house divided against itself will not stand" (Matt. 12:25).

The Bible further illustrates the value of a team: "Two are better than one, Because they have a good reward for their labor. For if they fall, one will lift up his companion. . . . A threefold cord is not quickly broken" (Eccl. 4:9–10, 12). You can tell people to quit attacking each other and start working together. But how do you reverse those bad communication habits and bring about lasting change? Here are some practical suggestions from Dr. Fowler's years of family counseling experience. As you read, put a plus by those recommendations you currently follow in your marriage and a check by those areas that need improvement.

___ Realize and remind yourself often, "I can't change my partner, I can only choose to allow the Holy Spirit to change me and leave my spouse in God's hands. I can share an *I feel* or an *I'd like* message with my spouse, but I realize that my ultimate peace and joy cannot depend on how my spouse responds to me." If we share *I demand* messages, we are setting up the relationship for failure because no one can meet our every demand.

___ Take into consideration the 20–60–20 rule of thumb when involved in a relationship: About 20 percent of everything you do will be an irritant to your spouse, and 20 percent will automatically please your mate immensely. The rest of your behavior will fall in the middle 60 percent where you can influence your spouse's positive response through observation and practice. Delivery, tone of voice, timing, and body language are as important as the message conveyed. In his practice Dr. Fowler finds that too many spouses find it very convenient to fall into the negative 20 percent rather than work on the 60 percent!

___ If your spouse has a blind spot in a certain area, accept the shortcoming rather than directing your behavior according to what you feel your spouse should do. Try to picture him or her in a hospital bed. In a real life situation your spouse would be unavailable to you physically, yet you would still be married. Likewise, in a psychological sense there are areas where your mate is handicapped and is fairly unavailable to meet your needs. Yet you are still married. To be mentally healthy you need to be careful not to think constantly of *what ought to be;* rather, live in light of *what is.*

___ This simple listening activity is helpful for couples who find themselves in the habit of attacking each other: Repeat what your spouse says before making a comment. Many wives complain that their husbands or children do not listen to them. If a wife habitually interrupts or finishes the sentence for her husband, however, he may choose to detach himself. Or on the other extreme, he may become angry and lash out. Waiting for your spouse to finish and restating what he says tends to defuse the time bomb.

____ People who are really listening begin to be more sensitive and aware of their partner's deeper self. Attacking each other usually stems from poor self-esteem and insecurity. At the clinic we stress the need for couples to become "one," illustrating that attacking each other is comparable to members of an athletic team fighting each other instead of the opponent. Every member of such a team will end up losing, of course. The problem at hand should be the focus as we join forces with our spouse to find solutions.

____ Learn when to keep quiet. Judgmental attitudes and faultfinding can destroy unity. Arguments feed on blame like mold on moisture. There will constantly be a temptation to prove yourself right and someone else wrong. But remember that you don't always have to be right—sometimes it's enough just to be quiet! Consider L. L. Levinson's witty definition of *discretion:* "Putting two and two together and keeping your mouth shut."

____ When couples do come up with a solution to a problem, it is wise to say, "This seems best. Let's try it to see if it works." Sometimes when a solution becomes set in cement before it has been proven, more trouble results. Flexibility is a major characteristic of successful people and marriages.

The attitude of our family members will be a determining factor in how well we handle the stressful circumstances. Outlook affects outcome. Our attitudes can help or hinder the team effort. As William Raspberry, a columnist for the *Washington Post*, was quoted in *Reader's Digest:* "When people believe that their problems can be solved, they tend to get busy solving them.

On the other hand, when people believe that their problems are beyond solution, they tend to position themselves so as to avoid blame."[1]

Your Part of the Team Effort

You alone can change your attitude. Even though teamwork is a tremendous blessing, you are ultimately responsible for doing your part, and it is up to you to avoid focusing on what someone else should change.

Have you ever felt as if you were in the audience, watching life's drama from a distance? If so, then you can identify with the need to shake the theatrical illusions and to proactively participate in shaping the end of the story. The script is not yet complete. You have to take the initiative to lead your life toward a happy ending. *People who fail to recognize their own capacity and responsibility to make choices can waste their lives waiting because they believe that they must be helped from the outside.*

It is best to take responsibility for our own emotions and separate our response to the crisis from the reactions of those around us, even when we choose to unite with family members to face the problem. This is where Patti was getting tripped up. She found it difficult to distance herself and her outlook from Mike's moodiness and depression: "When Mike is having a bad day it sort of rubs off on the rest of us. I feel like the kids and I are the victims of his sour attitude."

The challenge is to recognize another's behavior for what it is—a reaction to stress, possibly, or a reflection of his or her mood—and think before we respond. Then we are less likely to get caught up in the emotional climate the other person creates. In seeking to sympathize it is possible to become enmeshed with another, or overly influenced by their emotional reactions. For maintaining psychological health and acting in everyone's best interest, a good rule to remember is "unite—but be careful not to merge." Choose your attitudes and actions.

And choose your close friends carefully. Not everyone is a constructive member of your team. When you are on a tightrope of stress, it pays to watch your step. Actively seek out relationships with those who can help you steady yourself. It may also be wise to temporarily distance yourself from nonsupportive people—it's hard enough to balance yourself without someone bouncing the rope! Don't feel guilty about pulling away from draining individuals whose help is no help.

Also ask yourself: Am I on my own team or am I working against myself? Although the question may sound strange, you may discover that you are actually at odds with yourself in a crisis situation. Relentlessly blaming yourself or mentally criticizing past and present behaviors will subvert your ability to respond with poise and confidence. This critical inner voice can be activated in any vulnerable situation.

Counteractive thoughts often include negative forecasts about one's ability to handle the future. Instead, refuse generalized self-criticism. You need to nurture and encourage yourself—be your own friend! A person in an adversarial relationship with himself can not properly relate to others. The individual fighting an inner war with God faces the same stumbling block.

Do you feel as though God is on your side? One young mother who had been struggling to make ends meet during long months when her husband's business faltered remarked, "When a major bill came, an unexpected and outrageous insurance adjustment, I found myself thinking, *Don't you love me, God?* I was surprised by the intensity of my reaction and realized I was plugging into some unresolved feelings. I was angry at God, doubting His love and wisdom, and feeling that I deserved better. That anger was spilling over into other relationships."

WHEN TO ASK WHY

There are times when it is important and wise to ask why something has happened to you. There is some value in retracing your steps and asking yourself: *How did I arrive in this situation? Did poor decisions contribute to the mess I'm in now? Did my pain result from someone else's behavior, and if so is there any way I can prevent exposing myself to this again in the future?*

Turn your trial into a learning situation. But remember, the purpose of looking back is to gain insight and wisdom—not to lay on guilt. It is helpful to admit where we were wrong or to acknowledge that we are suffering because of someone else's sin. This, too, is facing reality. Constantly focusing on who is to blame for what has happened, however, is counterproductive.

By looking back, Mike and Patti realized that their situation was more complicated because they had inadequate savings to fall back on. Rather than pointing fingers at who had spent too much, they simply chose to learn from their mistake and avoid repeating it. They resolved to continue some of their cutbacks in expenditures even after Mike found employment in order to eliminate their debt and put aside more rainy day savings. In order to be happy, the Carlsons had to accept their circumstances regardless of who was or was not at fault and shift the focus of their energy to improving those things that could be changed.

Some things can not be changed or avoided. And some things are no one's fault.

When any crisis occurs, it is natural to get caught up in the questions. "Why did it happen?" "Why did God allow our family to go through this?" "Why doesn't He do anything to change the situation?" It is understandable to cry out in honest pain, "Why me, Lord?" But we impede forward movement when we remain fixed in a state of anger and rebellion against God and our trials.

Rita remembers the questioning period:

Looking back on the time immediately after our daughters' illnesses were diagnosed, Arlan and I found no comfort in dwelling on the questions, Why do innocent children suffer? Why our little babies? Still the questions entered our minds, and we separately came to the same counterquestion. Why *not* our children? We live in a fallen world where suffering, disease, and sorrow are an inescapable part of life. No one is immune. No one is too young to die. Only in heaven, where God's will is perfectly done, are we promised a life with no more death or mourning or crying or pain (Rev. 21:4).

It was not the time to dwell on Why? The more important questions for her were *what* questions: What can we do to handle the stress in constructive ways? What choices have we made that are making matters worse? and What decisions can we make now to improve them? What can we learn in this situation? This change of focus is helpful. Pause here long enough to answer these questions as they relate to your family.

It also helped us to realize that our normal responsibilities as parents hadn't changed—we were to love and care for our children. And we tried not to let caring for their medical needs overshadow caring for their normal emotional and developmental needs. When we asked ourselves what we should do, we came up with very straightforward answers: Love our children. Be there when they need us. Pray for them. From that perspective we were able to maintain some order and balance in our lives even in a difficult situation.

In the same way, it may be necessary for you to look past your need to know *why* and to choose to respond to the needs of other family members. This is not meant to imply that you must deny your own pain or stuff your feelings. But just as an athlete may choose to play in a championship game despite an injury, there are times when life demands that we participate while in pain because the stakes are high. As we reach out to meet the needs of others we often find, in retrospect, answers to our own troubling questions.

When you think about *what* to do, also consider what it is best *not* to do. There are occasions when you need to help someone or accept help and other times when you should not. If you rush in and do for others what they can and should do for themselves, it robs them of a sense of achievement and control over their lives. Accepting such help can breed feelings of powerlessness, embarrassment, helplessness, and despair.

Arlan and I felt extremely helpless at times because we couldn't heal our daughters or make their pain go away. Yet the medical problems our children faced caused us to reevaluate our lives and cherish our children more. We've grown more grateful for our children and our heavenly Father. Facing the possibility of losing our little ones drew our attention to what love and health and life really are. Privileges. Gifts. Blessings!

As we go on to look at the typical response patterns of people in crisis, keep in mind that life's tough times can result in new insights, greater appreciation, and closer relationships.

5

Drawing the Line

Typical Response Patterns of People in Crisis

Helen awoke in the night to find her husband, Jim, unconscious in the bathroom, sitting with his back against the wall. His color was ashen, his breathing raspy and labored. She whispered a prayer as she put in a call to the local rescue squad. As she did, Helen heard Jim's voice from behind her, asking what she was doing.

Helen recalls, "I was stunned to see him standing there nearly normal after seeing him looking so ghastly in the bathroom just moments before. I told Jim I was calling the rescue squad, and he ordered me to put down the phone—he did *not* need their help! Any attempt to persuade him to see a doctor, then or in the days to come, was just a waste of time. He was adamant about not having medical help.

"Life went on almost normally for the next two months as Jim slowly regained his strength and began to resume his farming chores," Helen explains. "His health began to deteriorate, however, and he became an old man before my eyes. I was helpless to do anything about it. Those were very stressful days. He had chosen his own destiny and refused any counsel to the contrary."

Helen describes emotional responses with which we can all identify. What we do to handle stressful demands will, of course, vary according to a number of factors. Although there are too many influences to consider them all in one book, we can all relate to general behaviors. As you read through the reactions described below, check those that mirror your own response to crisis.

WHAT TO EXPECT

The chart on page 70 shows the basic steps on the path from a shock event to resolution. If you face a crisis, it gives you a general idea of where you are headed.

While you read Helen's account, consider her response behaviors as the melody line of a life temporarily thrown into a minor key—a main theme that has countless variations. Listen for these strains in your own relationships.

When Jim refused to see a doctor, Helen struggled with many emotions. She remembers, "During those days I knew in my heart that something was going to happen to my husband. . . . I didn't really believe he would die and yet a part of me prepared in practical ways for that possibility. . . . This was a time of great

What Happens When a Crisis Occurs?

Here's what to expect.

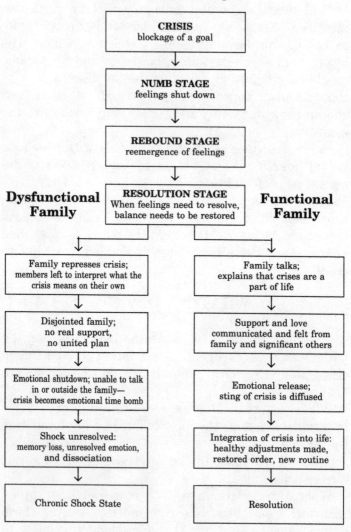

anxiety, not knowing from day to day if something was going to happen. I wondered, *How could I help? How could I plan? Should he even be driving?* During the night I always listened for the labored breathing of another attack. I began to let go of him in little ways, trying to stay positive and yet realistic.

"And so it was with a form of relief that I greeted the end of the suspense when his death did come. He died in the church that he loved among caring friends and a loving pastor. He was taken out of this world without a struggle or any suffering, just as he would have designed it himself. At that moment the arms of God were around me, granting me total peace and control. . . . I had less stress then than at any time during the two months before. The strain of uncertainty was over."

Numbness

Perhaps the most predictable response following a crisis event is a period of numbness. And if the event has been preceded by a difficult period of waiting or uncertainty, there is often a paradoxical sense of relief when reality replaces anxiety.

Doctors have discovered that during a time of extreme crisis, our body often produces a drug similar to Valium. This is why Helen initially felt numb. It is common for a person to notice a decreased sensation of pain in the first few days or weeks, saying things like, "I can't believe this is happening to us. It all seems so unreal—like a bad dream that I can't wake up from." Or if they believe in God, they may refer to this period as one of "total peace" as Helen did.

A person who is still under the influence of what one woman described as "God's emotional Novocain" may smile bravely and hold up well. Friends comment that "he's doing so well" and go back to their normal routine. Later, reality sets in and the person spirals downward emotionally, spiritually, or physically. Puzzled friends remark, "But he was doing so well. What happened?" Relationships may suffer if this delayed reaction is misunderstood.

Sensitivity and Overreaction

After an initial stage of shock, one can expect to go through a rebound stage. In this stage there is a reemergence of feeling to the point of oversensitivity. Overreacting to a remark, being touchier than usual, or taking things too personally are signposts of such a response.

Helen recalls, "In the days that followed Jim's death, the greatest stress came from well-meaning friends, acquaintances, and relatives. They gave me their genuine condolences. But in the majority of cases, they added, 'And you don't drive, do you?' For years I'd had strong negative feelings about learning to drive, and their comments made me feel like a dummy because I didn't know how and had no desire to learn. I needed their love and understanding; instead, their remarks lowered my self-esteem and made me feel inferior. I now recognize that at the time of bereavement, any sensitive issue becomes more sensitive than ever—and learning to drive was the subject where I felt most vulnerable."

Identity Shifts

Like Helen, most people find their sense of identity and self-esteem to be vulnerable following a significant hardship, whether it is medical, financial, or interpersonal. A person under pressure becomes increasingly sensitive to the perceptions and judgments of others.

This can be a time of shifting identity. The individual may begin to act out a drama that can last for years, using roles picked up quickly in crisis. Those with a strong established social network before the crisis are less susceptible to the problem.

For years Helen had relied on Jim's take charge personality and responsible nature. Looking back, she says she was "crippled by kindness" in some ways. Switching from the role of being taken care of to that of handling all the financial, business, and daily decisions of life was made more difficult by her inexperience in these areas. But she successfully adjusted to her new role with a positive resolve to manage her life well.

As with Helen, the willingness to take on new roles and the shedding of old ones often opens the door to personal growth and constructive change. On the other hand, the refusal to accept the changes brought about through crisis can render a person ineffective the remainder of her life.

Grieving the Loss

Death is not the only loss people may experience. Frustrations, disappointments, crippling handicaps, and divorce are losses. The loss of jobs, dreams, health, or community—all must be appropriately worked through and grieved. Not everyone goes through all five stages of grief (denial, anger, bargaining, depression, and guilt) before acceptance comes, but each stage poses its own potential threat to relationships. Each person handles grief differently and on a different timetable.

Examine the things that have happened and are happening now in your life. What are the major losses you have experienced? How have these been handled? Did the people around you encourage you to talk through feelings and grieve in a healthy way? If not, can you identify unresolved issues from past losses that you need to work through? Rita remembers a sense of numbness followed by a feeling of inner rage at a world gone wrong:

I was angry at a world where babies had to suffer, where people slowly deteriorated from cancer, where families were torn by events outside their control. And I was angry at God for not putting a stop to it all! Although I accepted the anger as a normal part of the adjustment to loss, many of my Christian friends felt it was sinful to be angry with God and a poor testimony to admit it. They couldn't understand that, to me, trusting God's love meant believing I could be honest with Him. I figured there was no use pretending—God already knew what I was really thinking! My anger pushed me toward prayer, not away from God.

I also remember wishing I could somehow trade places with the girls; they were so innocent, and it seemed unfair that they should have to suffer. But I didn't really bargain with God because I didn't believe He operated that way. During the times when I was especially tired I struggled with depression and despair.

To a lesser degree I passed through the denial, anger, bargaining, depression, and guilt stages in response to a host of little losses—the loss of leisure time, the loss of financial comfort, the loss of control over my schedule. I remember feeling guilty because I wanted to spend money on a vacation from everything rather than on medical bills.

Helen recognized how the grieving process was affecting her relationships and made wise adjustments. "Anger was my biggest hurdle," she comments. "Not anger at God but anger at my husband for dying. Does that make sense to be angry at him? Well, in one way it doesn't have to make sense. Jim could have sought medical attention, thus possibly prolonging his life.

"I held in my hurts and anger toward others for their remarks concerning my learning to drive until my brother came along, expressing exactly the same sentiments. My veneer burst and I blew up! All the pent-up emotions poured out onto him, creating a temporary rift. It was up to me to apologize and he graciously accepted. Only others who had grieved over a loss could understand how a simple statement could be so blown out of proportion. Eventually I became more tolerant and more understanding of my own sensitivity. But I had to do a lot of praying about this issue."

When we are adjusting to significant losses, it helps to know that the grieving period may last 1 1/2–2 years. In his counseling, Dr. Fowler has noticed that it takes several *life cycles* for the sting of the loss to be lessened. Places, times, and events open the wound—that first Christmas and birthday that bring back deep memories or the radio playing "your song" or even just a dinner where his or her favorite food is served.

To ease the grieving process, plan to be with friends or relatives to start new memories during holidays and visits to sentimental places. The tendency is to withdraw from others at these times. This prolongs the cycle of adjustment, however.

Because the early grieving process is usually marked by extremes, friends and relatives should keep in mind that finding balance may take a while and not take behavior during this time too seriously. The tendency is to isolate yourself from others or to become overly dependent, so try to establish a social routine that adds stability—for example, church every Sunday, lunch with a friend on Tuesday, dinner with relatives every other Friday.

Affectional Attachments

People who are walking the tightrope of a crisis crave close relationships. Unfortunately these people often develop a random search and attach pattern; that is, they will feel, act and signal to others a readiness—in fact, a need—to latch on and hold on to those around them. Clinicians often experience demanding desire for closeness from distressed individuals.

This yearning for contact can put people who lack close friends at risk. Because of the intense desire for intimacy, it is especially important to seek out friends of the same sex during stressful times. It is also important to guard against undue emotional dependency on caregivers, therapists, doctors, and pastors.

The craving for understanding and affection does not need to be a negative factor, however. It can also create close friendships, bond families together during hard times, and deepen our relationship with God. For Helen the need surfaced in an appreciation of physical affection. "The most constructive support I received upon the death of my husband was found in the hugs of so many. There is so much healing to be found in the sense of touch."

Preoccupation with the Situation

When involved in a crisis, a person typically becomes preoccupied with the situation at hand. During every idle moment his mind is on the problem. The individual's attention, and therefore the topic of conversation, is focused on the crisis (this has been called the *topic-of-choice* phenomenon).

This preoccupation often leads to an extreme self-consciousness that affects extended relationships. "Sometimes I think casual acquaintances are thinking about our situation when actually they are not," one man remarked after the death of his teenage son.

It is perfectly appropriate, of course, for a person to give a great deal of thought to major events that change his life. Everyone will dwell on problems when a crisis is at hand! But a balanced look at life requires moving past the brooding stage to the resolving stage. Most often this must be done by deliberate choice.

Helen took a wise approach. "Letting others listen and help when there is something they can do builds loving relationships. During the grieving process I allowed people to minister to me," she explains. "But I continued on with my usual activities so that life would contain some degree of normalcy and relationships would be maintained. As time went on I became more and more involved in volunteer work, doing something of value for someone else so as not to become self-centered. I believe that it is through helping others that you help yourself the most."

Cloudy Decision Making

Not everyone will be capable of making the wise decisions Helen made, especially at first. Most will find that the ability to concentrate, memory, and decision-making skills shift into low gear after the intense demands of the crisis are past. Intense emotional reactions to trauma are centered in the right side of the brain, but rational thinking requires a switch to the left side of brain. Therefore, individuals reacting to emotional stress often exhibit cloudy, subjective reasoning.

And a person under extreme pressure often resorts to an exaggerated trial and error method of dealing with events. He may be willing to consider a large number of potential solutions but unable to sort and select among them. Family members, friends, and therapists are likely to influence the course of action eventually selected.

Those same significant others may also experience a

tremendous amount of frustration! When the individual you seek to comfort fails to act on advice or implement a plan of action, it is easy to get upset. Being aware that the decision-making process may be temporarily impaired following situations of high stress can ease the tension.

Carefully consider the checklist of typical response behaviors to crisis situations:

____ Numbness
____ Sensitivity and Overreaction
____ Identity Shifts
____ Grieving the Loss
____ Affectional Attachments
____ Preoccupation with the Situation
____ Cloudy Decision Making

List any of these responses that have played a role in your relationships over the past year. If the thought of getting it all on paper seems too overwhelming, try to find a supportive friend who will listen as you work through the details out loud. Just talking things through can clarify your thoughts. A word of caution: *Be sure to exercise discretion when you discuss sensitive issues.* It is easy to get hurt or to be misunderstood when your emotions are vulnerable.

THE NEXT STEPS

Not all tension will be avoided. Not all emotional pain can be bypassed. You can realistically expect to have good and bad times, closeness and friction. Dr. Fowler often draws the following line to represent gradual progress toward resolution and recovery. Rather than the single straight line of a tightrope that connects two points in the shortest distance, *recovery from a shock event generally consists of gradual progress interspersed with temporary setbacks.*

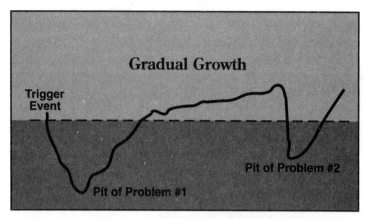

The upward slant of the line illustrates the movement toward relationship goals. Progress is being made. The V-shaped dips represent low times—the temporary setbacks and crisis moments. Don't give up if you slip a few times. Notice that the emotional pit on the right is actually *higher* than the starting point, so progress has been made even though it may feel as if all the gain has been lost in moments of despair.

Now that you have a general idea of where you have been and what to expect ahead, the next chapter lists some practical steps you can take to regain your balance.

6

One Step at a Time

Drawing Up a Working Plan

In the children's storybook *Alice's Adventures in Wonderland,* Alice eventually arrives at a crossroad of several paths. She feels frustrated, discouraged, and frightened. And she is confused by difficult circumstances that make no sense. Alice desperately wants to go back to where things return to normal. But she does not know where to go or what to do next.

Then the Cheshire Cat arrives on the scene and Alice asks, "Would you tell me, please, which way I ought to go from here?"

"That depends a good deal on where you want to get to," said the Cat.

"I don't much care where—" said Alice.

"Then it doesn't matter which way you go," said the Cat.[1]

Where Do You Want to Go: The Long Look

We're sure that Jerry, a stocky, dark-haired man in his midtwenties, could identify with Alice. The last time Rita and Arlan saw him, he ambled in and slouched on the chair, tapping his fingers on the edge of his worn-out tennis shoe. Then he launched into his current problems—he had moved again, in search of a better place to build relationships, and was now short on both money and friends.

Rita and Arlan hadn't seen Jerry in nearly a year, and he was still in the same state. Like Alice in Wonderland, he didn't much care where he went in life as long as he got out of his present troubles.

Jerry was just floating, appearing content to fall into whatever might happen. "I want to be totally available for anything God wants me to do," Jerry explained. In truth, Jerry was trying to duck the responsibility of decision making.

As a result of this lack of direction and discipline, Jerry lived in a state of *chronic crisis*. One problem always seemed to lead to another without resolution as he repeated the same mistakes in his interactions with others. Somehow he never mustered the healthy resolve to say, "I'll never do that again" and then follow through.

In a healthy relationship, many boundaries are already firmly in place before a disturbing event triggers stress, and they serve to give direction in difficult times. For example, long before Mike Carlson lost his job, Mike and Patti had made a commitment that the word *divorce* would never be mentioned—no matter how heated any argument became or how difficult things were. And they would not tolerate any physical abuse. Therefore, when difficult circumstances rocked their relationship, they wandered only so far off course. They came up against the solid fence of agreement and previous commitment. Although they were not sure what they *would* do, it helped that they knew for certain what they would *not* do. They had healthy hedges.

Jerry, on the other hand, lacked the security of guideposts. Like many people who lack interpersonal boundaries and personal aspirations, Jerry had not determined where he was headed and set some goals to get there.

Wanting to maintain stable relationships in a crisis without making deliberate decisions is like wanting to ride a bike without pedaling. To improve any relationship and to move toward resolution, you must choose a destination and then map out a way to get there. You must have a plan that looks beyond the present problems to be solved and focuses on the ultimate goal to be reached. If you fail to plan, you are planning to fail by default.

THE FLIGHT PLAN

In working toward his pilot's license, one of the first things Dr. Fowler learned was how to write a flight plan. Before the plane ever leaves the ground, a pilot makes decisions about the cruising altitude, route, destination, fuel on board, and alternate airport. The plan is meant to keep the pilot on course regardless of reduced visibility, mountain terrain, or adverse weather conditions.

When you set your heading to a certain degree, you fly to that. Flight instructors recommend that pilots locate a checkpoint in the first five minutes of a flight to make sure they are exactly on course. Dr. Fowler learned the hard way that if you wait for thirty minutes and then check, you might be twenty miles off already. He could not find the airport on his first cross-country trip and had to turn around and come back!

But with continued effort he learned how to keep on course. Having a flight plan is one of the preliminary steps basic to all aviation travel, and Dr. Fowler likes to use that metaphor when working with clients. If you want to keep your relationships on course during turbulent times, the same three steps apply.

1. Set a Specific Course

Choose one relationship that will be particularly beneficial to you in the days ahead and set a specific course. Ask yourself, *Where are we in this relationship? Where do we want to end up? How are we going to get there?* In other words, plan together the ways that you want to respond and the specific things you are going to do or not do. We strongly recommend that you put your plan in writing, and then place it where you can conveniently refer to it throughout the week. We will walk you through the process with the Schweitz family to get an idea of the kind of changes you can make in attitude, expectations, and conversation patterns to improve a relationship.

Arlan and Rita were dissatisfied with their relationship with their daughter Martha's medical specialist. They realized they were often frustrated by the doctor's words, even though they openly communicated with him. As they considered the frequent changes in the diagnosis and planned tests, they recognized that they were taking the doctor's words as concrete answers to their questions. The doctor, however, was only offering his best educated guess, which changed daily with additional information from test results.

Rita and Arlan easily came up with a plan to reduce the tension in the relationship. First, they would not set themselves up to be let down by hanging on the doctor's every word but would instead take a more relaxed, "wait and see" attitude. Second, they would not inform friends or family members and raise any expectations until they were sure, avoiding the embarrassment and bother of calling everyone back to explain. And third, whenever it seemed necessary, they would simply ask the specialist more questions rather than making assumptions that often proved incorrect. This simple plan improved their working relationship.

Now it's your turn. Read back through the first paragraph in this section and write out your flight plan. What changes can you make in attitude, expectations, and conversation patterns to improve your relationship? Put specific objectives and goals down on paper. As you think through your flight plan, keep in mind the following factors.

Determine a time frame to identify specific beginnings and endings. This provides a sense of closure in what might otherwise seem to be a never-ending struggle. Counseling experience has shown repeatedly that women especially benefit from setting time limits. Suppose your spouse suggests, "I feel it would be best if you worked fewer hours for the next few weeks." To build trust and deepen your relationship, place the request within a given time frame. Don't respond, "I'll try to take some time off when things slow down." Instead, give specifics: "My current project is on a tight schedule. But starting next Thursday I can cut out the overtime hours." Then keep your word.

Ask what you can *accomplish* with what you have, instead of what you can not do because of your limitations. Be resourceful. Don't let yourself fall into "If only I had (such and such) or he would do (what I want) then I could make the changes needed and handle things better." Begin *where you are* to do *what you can* with *what you already have.* Improvise!

With limited time and money, Arlan and Rita couldn't go out for dinner or a date each week to spend quality time alone. And they had to give up many leisure activities. Instead, they took more late night walks together after the kids were sleeping. These minibreaks provided conversation time and a chance to unwind from the day. Their relationship was strengthened within the limits of their circumstances.

In contrast, Jerry responded to stress with the vague belief that God's best for Him must be out there somewhere, but always in circumstances other than those he was in. This kept him from settling on a role he could fill or actions he could take *right now.* His response to problems was always to run. Jerry was also hindered by another misconception. He equated freedom with the absence of goals. But balanced, healthy relationships need direction and commitment to survive—with or without situations that bring additional restrictions.

Set up small goals for things you are going to do and take action. Choose self-discipline over self-pity. Don't attempt to leap tall buildings in a single bound—take the stairs. Even if you must take tiny steps, keep moving toward your goal. Just do the next thing. Then the next. If you can not find a staircase over the obstacles you face, don't assume a superman stance and take the heroic leap. Instead, enlist the help of friends to brainstorm a little. Maybe there is a way you can take a taxi to the other side!

Mike and Patti Carlson were having frequent arguments. But they didn't just decide to get along and avoid all conflict. Instead they set up small goals for handling conflict: Listen without interrupting. Don't raise your voice. Use sentences beginning with *I feel* or

I think things would go better if instead of confrontational *you should* statements. Attack the problem not each other.

Be practical and specific as you are setting your course. Keep in mind that your usual plan and habits of response may not always work during a crisis. Don't burden yourself with unrealistic goals or behaviors. On one very difficult day Rita commented to Arlan, "My head aches, my body aches, and my eyes burn. What do you think I should take?"

"A nap," he responded. "That is, a nap would be the obvious answer under normal circumstances. But since that's not an option, I guess you'll have to settle for plan B—take two aspirins with a Diet Pepsi!"

Stick with it. If you are looking for a reason to quit, you will find one. Resolve to tackle one task at a time without procrastinating. As you whittle away at big problems, breaking them down into smaller ones, the course you should take will often become clearer. Patterns of conversation can be particularly difficult to alter, but if you make a consistent effort you can learn more effective styles of communication.

2. Use Checkpoints

Make yourself accountable to each other. Are you doing what you said you were going to do? Having goals and guidelines does little good if no one follows them. Is your relationship still on course? Or have you drifted into the areas you meant to avoid? Check early. Check often. By setting these minicheckpoints you can avoid having to make major readjustments.

If your flight plan is specific, it includes reflection points at which you can stop and reaffirm each other. "We've made it this far." "We're handling things the way we set out to." "We're doing okay for the most part, but we need to do better at staying calm."

Be realistic. Even if you have to settle on a plan that is less than ideal, there is a sense of satisfaction when you successfully arrive at a checkpoint and celebrate the fact that you have covered some difficult ground together. During Rita and Arlan's darkest days, their goal was simply *endurance with stability.* They were so emotionally and physically exhausted that they gave themselves permission to just maintain. There were no thoughts of keeping sufficient romance and fun in their marriage—it was enough of a challenge to be patient and kind to one another! In the same way, your flight plan may be temporarily reduced to the grim resolve not to crash. When things let up a little you can get back on the course you have charted.

Having a flight plan with specific checkpoints for responses and communication will help restore some sense of control and order during times of trouble. But we need to qualify our recommendations by adding that not everyone lacks direction like Jerry. There are those who tend toward the opposite extreme. They not only take charge of directing their lives, but organize yours and everyone else's, too—if you let them!

Avoid either imbalance. The controlling person's flight plan includes steps to change the compulsive need for order. Specific steps might include: Don't make someone else's decisions. Resist perfectionism. Refuse to manipulate or bully people into compliance with your plan.

Here's another word of caution. Don't be like one couple who came into Dr. Fowler's office. He instructed the woman, "I want you to be thinking about what you would like your husband to do to help resolve this problem, and bring back your specific ideas next time." The next week she brought a list of forty-eight things she felt her husband should change! Dr. Fowler said, "Ma'am, that's admirable. But what *two things* do you want to work on this week?" Implement your flight plan one leg of the journey at a time. Be realistic.

3. Stay Calm, Cool, and Collected

In order to be effective, your flight plan should have some general, easy-to-recall objectives as well as specifics for problem areas. Any attempt to describe a single plan would be misleading—no two individuals are the same, and problems can not be solved by some magic formula. Even so, we have found the three C's approach, based on the cliché "stay calm, cool, and collected," to be effective. Check your attitude and actions against these goals:

Stay calm. When you encounter negative circumstances, you may feel anxious and will often become more irritable than usual. But maintaining your composure and an inner calmness will help. This tranquility should not be based upon feelings or external factors.

Excitable, overreactive people often jeopardize the stability of their relationships by hysterical or exaggerated responses. In contrast, a poised and calm individual is more resourceful and productive at problem solving. Pam, an energetic young woman who tended to dramatize everything, found that her friends became less sympathetic or avoided her during difficult times. When she asked a close friend why, the friend replied, "Because you always make such a big deal out of everything. It sometimes seems as though you just want attention—you don't want to calm down enough to listen to anything I say."

Together the women set two goals that helped. First, Pam was to make herself leave her hands quietly at her side and converse without dramatic gestures. Second, when Pam's voice went up in pitch, she was to mentally remind herself, *Take it down a notch.* If Pam did not slow down and steady her voice, her friend agreed to remind her. With practice and accountability Pam gained composure and a calmer style of communication.

Stay cool. Don't be easily angered. Angry outbursts and heated conversations are seldom constructive. As Dr. Fowler often tells his clients, "Refuse to put a thousand dollar price tag on dime store discouragements." When we are already under stress, the tendency is to respond to minor inconveniences as if they were of major consequence. We may get blistering mad at the doctor for being late for rounds or upset with the receptionist for putting us on hold.

A key to being mentally healthy is to put the proper price tag on events. Everything is not of equal value. In recovery therapy this is often one of the first beliefs that has to be changed. If everything that goes wrong is worth an extremely angry reaction, you will be up and down like a yo-yo. For a more balanced approach, make it your goal to stay cool and think clearly.

Stay collected. If you are in a crisis situation or anticipate a disturbing life event in the near future, now is the time to collect your act. Simplify your schedule and consolidate your efforts. Avoid fragmentation. Stress occurs when our responsibilities extend beyond our resources. So it is advisable to drop any draining projects you can, trim out unmanageable obligations, and refocus your schedule to reflect healthy priorities. Also collect your thoughts and reason through things before responding. Be quick to listen, slow to speak.

To simplify things, Arlan and Rita generally let two families know how things were going and asked them to get the word out to others rather than calling several relatives and friends. In order to gather her thoughts, Rita wrote them down in a daily devotional journal. Arlan and Rita also *collected* themselves through daily Bible reading and times of quiet reflection.

We will take a look inside Rita's journal in the next chapter as we talk more specifically about God's part in your flight plan. You will also find suggestions on how to move toward a personal relationship with God and find the faith you need during life's tough times.

Things may not go smoothly the first few times you try your new flight plan. If you continue to work on implementation, evaluation, and communication, however, you can expect to improve your relational skills. Take heart. When Dr. Fowler first began to fly small planes, he had some pretty rough landings. Looking back, he now quips, "The first few times, my landings made me feel glad I was only renting that airplane!"

But then he got the feel of the controls, and it became increasingly natural to touch down gently. In the same way, it will become increasingly comfortable, even automatic, for you to think out a course of action and to follow through on your flight plan.

In *Happiness Is a Choice*, Dr. Frank Minirth and Dr. Paul Meier explain that part of a Christian counselor's task is to persuade the patient "to commit his life to the *correct course* for obtaining inner love, happiness, and peace. People get very set in their ways. Even when they have tried their ways for twenty or thirty years with no lasting results, they still cling to childhood behavior patterns."[2]

Ask for God's help as you choose to abandon ineffective responses in favor of the healthier attitudes and behaviors we have been discussing. Don't be like Alice in Wonderland, who lamented over a common problem: "I give myself good advice, but very seldom follow it."

7

Held Steady by Faith

Balance in Your Spiritual Life

Nick Stinnett and John DeFrain, two noted professors of family studies, conducted the largest study of strong families ever undertaken. They studied more than three thousand families in the United States and abroad. In *The Secrets of Strong Families*, they reported that spiritual wellness was one important secret to the success of the strong families in their research; these families survived crisis by drawing on spiritual resources. "Sometimes we have a hard time talking about the spiritual realm," Stinnett and DeFrain wrote. "We're embarrassed or cannot find the right words. And yet over and over again the strong families talked about an unseen power that *can* change lives, *can* give strength to endure the darkest times, *can* provide hope and purpose."[1]

During a visit with Professor DeFrain at the University of Nebraska, Rita asked if his most current research supported the findings in the book. "Yes," he quickly replied. "Whenever we study strong families, spiritual wellness—religion, faith, or whatever you want to call it—is brought up as a powerful and important source of strength."

Growing in your relationship with God can bring purpose, inner peace, strength under stress, and help for daily living. Yet some of you may be ready to slip ahead a few pages because you feel faith is a private matter. If you read on, however, you will find the suggestions made on the following pages are practical not pious.

TIMES OF QUIET REFLECTION AND PRAYER

One practical way many people satisfy their spiritual yearnings is to set aside fifteen to thirty minutes each day for prayer, meditation, or reflection. They use these moments to contemplate the nature of God and to fix their mind on His Word. Terry finds it particularly helpful to get away from the scene of stress, phones, and interruptions by taking a walk to enjoy the beauty of nature. "Stepping out of a dim, sterile hospital room and walking outside into a cool, fresh breeze is like shifting worlds. When I look up at the stars glittering in the night sky, I can't help but change my perspective. Nature provides such an awesome picture of the bigness of God that my problems shrink by comparison. For me, inner tranquility and peace are closely linked with the great outdoors."

For Ken it is music that prepares the way for prayer

and meditation during life's tough times. "Sitting down at the piano to play or listening to songs of praise and worship on the stereo quiets my heart and helps me listen to God. I tend to think about general theological concepts more than specific verses: God is wise. God is powerful. God loves me. Therefore this temporary trouble can not be designed to destroy me—instead, bearing up will perfect my character and bring honor to God. Something good will come of it, as God promises in Romans 8:28, 'We know that all things work together for good to those who love God, to those who are the called according to His purpose.'"

Contemplation inspired by magnificent works of art can also lead to spontaneous prayer. Perhaps the most common approach to prayer involves seeking out a quiet place that affords some privacy and simply talking to God: "Trust in Him at all times, you people; / Pour out your heart before Him; / God is a refuge for us" (Ps. 62:8). We can relate to God with complete honesty. Talking through even our most vulnerable or hostile feelings is safe with God. He already knows all about the situation and everything we are feeling. And God loves us deeply. Prayer is a heart-to-heart talk with our heavenly Father.

A balanced relationship with God involves not only praying but also listening for His answers and doing what He instructs. But we live in a world geared for people who are preoccupied with meeting the needs at hand. It is difficult to take time for solitude, silence, and prayer when our problems are whirling through our minds and twisting up our schedules. We must learn to listen in many ways. God speaks today through art, music, and the beauty of creation. If we will listen, God will make Himself heard when we read the Bible, when we respond in service, and when we interact with others.

"Be careful not to let your emotions get in the way when you listen to God," Dr. Fowler warns. Individuals in crisis may have premonitions about upcoming events, strong hunches, inner impressions, dreams, or highly emotional experiences that can be explained psychologically and may be misinterpreted as messages from God. Traumatized people must also guard against reading things into Scripture to support a desired outcome. As a safeguard, don't make impulsive, life-changing decisions based on isolated, subjective factors, and don't trust emotional leadings. If you feel God is telling you to do something, be sure to validate the message by checking it against biblical truth in a broader context and discussing it with trusted friends who are in a position to be more objective.

GOD'S WORD FOR THOSE WHO HURT

Sandra Aldrich, author of *Living Through the Loss of Someone You Love*, writes, "Even when supported by strong faith, we can still have moments when our human fears and emotions threaten us. During those times, I turn to my Bible for encouragement. I'm especially drawn to the Psalms, accounts of Jesus' ministry, and Old Testament stories of courage and victory. Sometimes the Lord uses one particular verse to encourage me. . . . As you ask the Lord's direction, He'll give you special verses too."[2]

The following are some of the Bible verses that helped Sandra, Ken, and others through moments of feeling confused, afraid, lonely, abandoned, tired, or overwhelmed. Start with those that apply to feelings you may be having:

Confused   **Afraid**

Psalm 32:8   John 14:27

Proverbs 3:5–6
Jeremiah 33:3
Philippians 4:6–7

Isaiah 41:10
Psalm 118:6–7
Joshua 1:9

Lonely

Matthew 5:4
Psalm 25:16–17
1 Peter 5:7
Psalm 34:18

Abandoned

Hebrews 13:5–6
Deuteronomy 31:6
Jeremiah 31:3
John 14:27

Tired

Matthew 11:28–30
Psalm 23
Jeremiah 31:25
Deuteronomy 1:31

Overwhelmed

Jeremiah 29:11
Psalm 27:13–14
Jeremiah 32:17, 27
Philippians 4:13

When you read the Bible, it is helpful to keep a pencil in hand to jot down thoughts or applications God is pointing out to you. And as Rita discovered the hard way, designating one notebook specifically for that purpose makes it much easier to keep track of your notes and refer to them later—napkins, scraps of paper, and old church bulletins are not ideal!

Keeping a Journal

A notebook for this purpose is also referred to as a *devotional diary* or *spiritual journal*. Writing down inspirational thoughts does not have to be time-consuming or elaborate. To move his clients toward a satisfying relationship with God, Dr. Fowler has them keep a journal. He gives these instructions for beginning a journal:

1. Put down the date.
2. Ask God to give you at least one insight today.
3. Jot down prayer requests, goals, or insights.
4. Read ten minutes or longer from the Bible. While

you read, look specifically for a helpful principle or one piece of the puzzle to your problem.

5. Meditate at least five minutes on what you have read. Relinquish to God a particular problem. Admit to Him your helplessness and ask Him to take control.

6. Write down one thought for the day.

In the language of the flight plan, God is the pilot who has delegated many responsibilities to you as co-pilot. Even during your hardest times, God is with you. As a pilot turns to a navigation log and to instruments for direction, you can turn to God's Word and to prayer. The Bible gives inspiration, comfort, and principles of wisdom to move you through troubled times safely. The journal helps you chart your course and check your bearing.

A man we will call Robert had been unfaithful to his wife. As a Christian, he felt convicted for breaking his code of morality, and he genuinely repented. But in the meantime his wife, Mary, found out about the former affair and separated from him. Robert tried to woo her back, but she didn't trust his change of attitude and repentant spirit. Robert became depressed and came in to see Dr. Fowler at the clinic. Dr. Fowler suggested he keep a journal and begin by picking a book of the Bible to read through sequentially, a chapter or so each day. Here is a sample of the journal entries Robert later shared with Dr. Fowler, to give you some ideas on how to begin your own notebook.

May 25

Prayer Requests: God, it was five months ago today that Mary left me. I want her back. I desire her companionship and her love. I'm lonely and feel like I'm not doing something right; otherwise, she would be back. Is my prayer ever going to be answered? Please give me relief.

Reading: John, Chapter 11

Meditation on Passage:

- Mary and Martha were upset that Jesus didn't come when they called for him. I'm upset that my Mary isn't coming back . . . I must be patient and wait for God's timing.
- Jesus didn't respond as Mary and Martha had requested. He chose an entirely different way to heal Lazarus. I need to allow God to heal our relationship His way. Like Mary and Martha, I can't understand the delay, yet it's comforting to know God still loves me.
- Jesus feels our pain as His own.
- In the case of Lazarus, Jesus resurrected him. If our marriage is to work, it needs to be resurrected as well! The old must be abandoned and we need to start a new life together.

Thought for the Day: Delay doesn't mean God doesn't hear—His timing may not be the same as my timing.

Three days later Robert jotted down these thoughts:

May 28

Prayer Requests: Dear Jesus, you know I am human. I have drives and unmet intimacy needs. Yesterday my old fling called to say she is still available. It's so tempting, yet I must not give in.

Why do others want me, Lord, and my wife
doesn't?

Reading for the Day: John 14

Meditation on Passage:

- The temptation to obtain momentary pleasure is
  not worth the misery it will bring me. Peace
  comes from obedience (v. 27). Rekindling a fling
  is the world's way to bring happiness.
- Jesus discusses heaven. The passage has forced
  me to see that eternity is forever—and my pain
  is but for a season. I've concluded that even if
  Mary doesn't come back, I will remain faithful.
- The key to having victory over my temptation is
  to work on my relationship with Jesus; I need
  reminders of His perspective.
- Jesus has promised to be close at hand if I abide
  in Him.

Thought for the Day: The principle I'm learning is
"I must let go of what I can't control!"

Robert's story has a happy ending. About a year
later Robert's wife came across his journal by accident.
She later told Dr. Fowler in a joint counseling session
that it was Robert's consistent journal entries that convinced her that he had indeed changed and really
wanted the marriage to work. They are now happily
and faithfully reunited.

Journal keeping makes us proactive instead of reactive. And it helps us realize that spiritual growth is
taking place. Without a journal it is more difficult to
track changes in attitude or behavior because the
change is so gradual. Dr. Fowler had been counseling
Lyle, a tall man in his late thirties, for several weeks
when Lyle became discouraged and said, "My personal

relationship with God is not getting anywhere." Dr. Fowler suggested they spend the session going over Lyle's journal. To his amazement, Lyle could see areas where growth had occurred. He then was able to deal with issues in positive ways where he had struggled before. By looking back, Lyle could see how God was working in his life.

Spiritual journals are as unique as the people who keep them. Evelyn Boswell, a homemaker in Plentywood, Montana, wrote an article about her discovery of the value of a journal of thanks. "Several years ago, after a particularly good day, I tried to make a mental list of everything good that had happened. I had trouble remembering it all, though, so I took out a sheet of paper and started writing. The longer I wrote, the more things came to mind. When I finished, I was amazed to see that even more good things had happened to me that day than I had realized.

"I saw God's working in 'circumstances' and 'coincidences' that ordinarily wouldn't have warranted a second thought," Evelyn continues. "All the things that had gone right that day far outnumbered the one or two things that had gone wrong. I saw much to be thankful for. Ever since that day I've kept a notebook where I list all the things I'm thankful for on a particular day. If I have a concern or a problem, I list it too. But over the years I've found that my 'thank you' lists are much longer than my 'problem' lists. My journal has shown me again and again the truth of Psalm 100:5: 'The Lord is good; His lovingkindness is everlasting, And His faithfulness to all generations.' "[3]

Rita's devotional journal was never as structured as Dr. Fowler's outline. Sketches, poems, songs, and parables were penciled in alongside Bible study notes and prayers. Here is a look inside:

July 11

"The end of a matter is better than its beginning"
(Eccl. 7:8).

I agree with God.

Sometimes it feels like nothing I do stays done, and there's no end to my to do list. I have to do the laundry, the dishes, and pick up toys again tomorrow. I think the process of writing this journal is more helpful to me than what I write. It makes me feel good to start something and then complete it—even if I'm only completing a sentence!

The end.

There were, of course, times when the entries were more serious, but the journal reflected a relationship with God that included times to laugh as well as times to cry, times to dance as well as times to kneel. Below we share a word picture comparing God's loving care to that of an earthly father, taken from Rita's journal.[4] But first Rita gives the background that led up to the entry in her journal.

One area of anxiety that I prayed about often was having two children in the hospital at the same time and not being able to be there for both of them. My journal records God's delightful faithfulness in answering my prayer. When Erin's heart problem was first detected, we were told that she would need surgery in a month. But when we returned to the hospital for follow-up tests with our bags packed to stay, Erin's condition had stabilized and the operation was postponed—which was good because we arrived at the hospital with Martha the next day! From then on Erin's hospital stays for angiograms and procedures to lower her blood count to a safe level always fell in between Martha's hospitalizations although there were other close calls before Martha's health improved.

When Erin was three and I was about six months into my third pregnancy, Erin's cardiologist felt we should go ahead with surgery. The surgery was scheduled in Rochester, Minnesota, for two weeks after my due date, but our baby didn't know he was due. Cale arrived ten days later than planned. So I was in the hospital recovering from the delivery when I needed to be packing. Then Cale began reacting to breast milk just as Martha had, and we left for the Omaha hospital with him immediately. No one had warned us that the rare digestive disorder could reoccur.

Because of our previous experience with Martha, the specialist consented to let us take Cale home on a prescribed feeding schedule with the same special formula. When we explained that we had to leave for Rochester, however, the doctor grew concerned. "There's a significant chance Cale will need to be hospitalized within the next week or two," he said.

That night was one of the lowest times we faced. We decided that Arlan would have to leave the following afternoon with Erin for the clinic appointment and blood tests, and I would try to come up with our newborn son three days later. We prayed that four-day-old Cale wouldn't be hospitalized in Rochester during Erin's surgery or in Omaha before we left.

The next morning when Erin's cardiologist called to say that he had cancelled Erin's surgery, we were stunned. Erin's doctor knew nothing of Cale's complications. Because of his concerns about a possible miscommunication between doctors, he had backed out of the surgery rather than take any chances. When I hung up the phone and told Arlan, we danced around the kitchen in glee then went out for pizza to celebrate! God had intervened again.

A few days later Cale was hospitalized as predicted. His condition improved rapidly, and he was released after a couple of weeks. When Cale was three months old, Erin had her first heart surgery. The journal I kept was the spiritual lifeline that pulled me through these struggles. Here is what I read in the Bible and wrote in my notebook following Erin's operation:

> *"Do not fear, for I am with you;*
> *Do not anxiously look about you, for I am your*
>   *God.*
> *I will strengthen you, surely I will help you,*
> *Surely I will uphold you with My righteous right*
>   *hand."*
>
> (Isa. 41:10 NASB)

The rattle of steel alerted us to a patient being wheeled from the recovery room to the pediatric intensive care unit. In the eternal twilight of the unit our tiny daughter looked anxiously about, her eyes wide with fear.

Erin lay defenseless, strapped to her bed in the confusing semiconsciousness that follows heart surgery. Needles and tubes invaded every appendage. Monitored for everything—except pain and fear, I thought.

Arlan moved swiftly into action when he saw her fear. He quickly rose and spoke, his voice choked with compassion. "Don't be afraid, Erin," he said softly. "It's OK; Mommy and Daddy are here now. We're not going to leave you."

As his voice soothed her, Arlan stretched his massive frame over the iron bed rails to cradle our fragile child. Bending around the infusion pump to draw his face down near hers, he stroked her hair back with one hand. He slid his other hand through the maze of tubes and restraints until it reached hers.

I watched as Erin's hand closed tightly around the single finger he had laid across her palm. Turning toward Arlan's voice, her eyes met his. A look of recognition and relief flooded her face, rinsing away the confusion and fear. She began to relax, but her eyes never left his, as she drew strength and security from our presence.

Over and over Arlan whispered, "Don't be afraid; we're here with you. We love you," until she drifted off to sleep. Only then did he slide back into the chair. I knew how his back must have ached from the strain of holding that position for nearly two hours. I also knew without a doubt that Arlan would be there for Erin when she awoke.

If an earthly father's love could make him long so intently to comfort his child, how much more must our Father in heaven long to help us now in our time of trouble? God is bending over us, aching to comfort and reassure us, waiting for us to turn toward His voice. Our Father loves us deeply. Instead of anxiously looking around, I need to fix my eyes on His face, to draw strength from His presence. Imitating Erin's faith in her daddy, I can hold on to my heavenly Father. He will never leave us.

You may not care to write complete stories in your journal as Rita did or to jot down how your behavior measured up against the biblical instruction as Lyle did. That's fine. Each person has the freedom to creatively reach out to God in his or her own way. But the message is the same: God will never leave you. God loves you and will help you when you turn to Him.

SEEING GOD'S LOVE IN ACTION

Seeing God's love in action will strengthen your faith and deepen your relationship with Him. Therefore we strongly encourage you to surround yourself with people who are living examples of God's love. Ask for prayer and support from someone who maintained solid relationships with God and others during a similar trial. If you have questions about prayer or deepening your devotional life, seek out a pastor or Christian friend who can tell you how Jesus can meet your daily needs.

It also helps to stay connected with a local church or small Bible study group. Get together with like-minded friends to laugh, have fun, and talk informally about spiritual matters. In the next chapter we will talk in greater detail about the role of the caring community and the encouragement provided by an extended support network.

8

The Balance Poles

Listening, Caring, and Sharing

"Danny was fourteen, and to us he was just about perfect. He was involved in basketball, wrestling, and track. He was president of student council, played first trumpet in the band, and was active in the church orchestra and the youth choir. He loved the Lord and wanted to go to the Air Force Academy after high school. We were really proud of him and enjoyed going to all the many activities to cheer him on. He was a good model of what you'd want your young teenager to be like, and a real joy to us," Danny's mother, Dale Mills, explained. "One afternoon Danny accidently shot himself while fooling around with a gun. It killed him instantly."

Danny's father added, "By the time I arrived home,

not only had the rescue squad and police come, but a lot of our friends had heard the tragic news and had come to support us. After hugging my wife and my remaining two children, we gathered as a family for prayer. I felt it was imperative that we pray as a family and bind Satan through Christ's power so that he would not have any power in our lives to bring guilt, discouragement, depression, or even death. And as testimony to Christ's power, we've seen our prayer answered during the past two-and-a-half years since Danny died."

THE COMMUNITY RESPONSE

Like Dan and Dale Mills, any family may be called upon to face a crisis very suddenly; a heart attack, an accident, a doctor's grim diagnosis, a crime, or any other traumatic event may occur without warning. Popular psychology and the mass media suggest in subtle and not so subtle ways that all problems can be solved quickly. In real life it doesn't work that way. The aftermath of a crisis is an intense, overwhelming, and often desperate time. The metaphor of being together on a tightrope was not chosen to be melodramatic. For many the crisis threatens their life, the life of their marriage, and the survival of their family.

Consider the sobering findings of a recent study conducted by the University of Nebraska that surveyed parents and grandparents in families where a child had died without warning from sudden infant death syndrome: "More than four in ten parents in our most recent study considered suicide because of the death [of their baby]. Living becomes almost unbearable for most. Mothers and fathers tell us of slitting their wrists, trying to kill themselves in an automobile crash, trying to overdose on drugs, turning the motor of the car on in a closed garage. . . . The responsibility falls to each of us in society to help in any way we can to serve these stricken people. They are clearly crushed in a life-threatening and spiritually numbing situation."[1]

Although the many variables affecting crisis responses differ depending upon the type of situation the family encounters, all the scientific research as well as case studies we considered point out one glaring consistency: *In times of crisis people need to know that others care.*

It is difficult if not impossible to make it alone. The first five days appear to be critical. To better understand the impact of support relationships and to determine the most helpful community response to individuals in need, we personally interviewed or surveyed more than fifty families who successfully handled tough times. Input from these individuals was added to insight gathered from Dr. Fowler's case studies over the past decade. Then we compared our findings with extensive research conducted by Professor DeFrain and others at the University of Nebraska. Regardless of the case study, research, or personal encounter we considered, three points were evident. We pass them on to you as the simplified basics of maintaining strong relationships with people who are facing a crisis.

1. *Making an immediate initial contact is essential,* even if simply to acknowledge that you are aware of and care about what has happened to them.
2. *Follow-up is a key factor.* Continued contact and communication, especially listening, is a significant element in loving relationships.
3. *Individualize your care.* Be patient with people and allow them room to grieve or respond differently.

There is a great need for us to care for one another in a loving, gentle, nonthreatening way during a crisis. Even if the traumatic events occur within our own family, we are still called to be part of the caring community for our spouse and children while we are seeking our own resolution. In the remainder of this chapter, we give specific, useful information on these three general guidelines that will help you learn how to say the right things, do what is perceived as a helpful gesture, and actively listen without draining yourself of the desire to be involved.

Making Immediate Initial Contact

When we hear that a friend is facing heartbreaking personal problems, intense emotions surface. Many of us are not comfortable with strong emotions and have not been taught to acknowledge our own feelings. Instead we do everything we can to keep life at arm's length and on an intellectual level. In our pleasure-focused society we are not conditioned to be receptive to someone else's pain. But making an immediate initial contact is a tremendous support to the distressed family.

If there is a strong show of support, the family or individual can take comfort in knowing their community is concerned about them, their friends will stand with them, and there are others who care deeply and share their pain. Dan and Dale Mills appreciated the community response to Danny's death. In many ways the manner in which the tragedy was handled was a picture of the healthy action of a caring body of people working together.

Dan recalls, "I know we probably had two or three hundred people who came that night to the house. And it seemed like every time somebody new would come, a wave of emotion would hit and maybe last for ten or fifteen seconds. It was difficult, but after those waves would wash over me I was left with a real peace from God. Those surges of emotion and tears were a kind of cleansing, a way of expressing my grief.

"Elizabethton, Tennessee, is not a particularly large town, but our friends and the community were wonderful. The outpouring from others went far beyond what we ever expected. Stores offered their services and people rallied around us—washing dishes, cleaning up, doing anything they could to help. A local pastor wrote an article acknowledging our loss with the message that bad things do happen to good people yet God is faithful. Over a thousand people either came to visit our home or the chapel or attended the funeral service."

Often we do not know what to say or how to help, so we just take the low road and duck the problem, never even mentioning the name of the person who was hurt or died. Many times we avoid those in distress for so long that we assume (incorrectly) that we can reenter the conversation as if nothing has happened—just picking up where we left off on safe subjects like work, weather, and world affairs. But doing everything we can to pretend as if nothing has happened has an adverse effect, leaving deep hurt feelings or an awkward strain on the relationship.

Dan remembers, "A few of Danny's teachers and people in our community have never spoken to us or even acknowledged Danny's death. They may not have known what to say, but their silence was much more painful. Sometimes we would see people come toward us and then turn away because they didn't know what to say or how to respond. This was very difficult to take. It's better to just go up to the person and tell them, 'I don't know what to say, but I care about you, I'm praying for you, and if there's anything I can do, let me know.' Normally we know people care about us, but during the grief process it seems that you need to be told more often."

Dr. Fowler agrees that it is best to let others know that you care. Tell them you are available if they want to talk. Be aware of your body language, the way you talk, your tone of voice. Eye contact will show your sincerity. If you recognize a need, offer specific help to give relief, but only if you are genuinely available to follow through. Simply ask how they are feeling and let them talk. Listen carefully to their feelings, fears, and concerns. If you are unable to be there in person or don't know the individual well enough to stop by, a personal note or card is always in good taste.

It takes a measure of maturity to override your personal feelings of discomfort and reach out to others in their time of need. "In today's society it seems like we're afraid of our emotions. And we do everything we can to hide them," Dan Mills observes. "But one of the first things I would encourage people to do is to just be there and express their love and concern openly. . . . That's what was so comforting to us, just knowing we had that support base."

Follow-up Is a Key Factor

As significant as the initial show of support is, nothing takes the place of continued contact and communication. Syndicated columnist Ann Landers, when she was keynote speaker for the National Convention of the American Association for Counseling Development, remarked, "The success of my column underscores for me one of the principle tragedies of our times: There are people out there who have no one to talk to."

When the people we surveyed were asked to mention nonsupportive responses they received from others, many reported a common theme—friends and family members were there in abundance at first, then absent later on when companionship would have been greatly appreciated. Few people were available to listen when they wanted to talk. As one woman put it, "Everybody went overboard to keep in touch, almost to the point of being pushy, during the first month. Then the calls and letters and visits dropped off sharply just when I was ready for consolation and conversation. Interaction went from one extreme to the other."

This lack of follow-up occurs for many reasons. People going through a difficult time are expected to be emotional at first. But then as the days go by, they often feel expected to get on with life. So they begin putting everyone else at ease no matter how they really feel. They appear to be getting along so well that others may think continued support is unnecessary. In reality individuals recovering from the initial crisis typically experience high times as well as very intense low times. They may be afraid to mention their true feelings or ask someone to come over for a heart-to-heart talk.

As caregivers we are usually eager to get things back to normal. We are often unrealistic about how long it takes to get over a crisis. The need to share with others and to talk to others who have gone through similar circumstances may last two years or longer. "As the days go by, few people talk about our son or ask how we are doing. . . . The need to talk about Danny seems to grow less but it will never go away. He was a real part of our life and we will never want to give that up," Dale explains. "I am a happy, fulfilled person, but everything that comes into my life will be sifted through my experience with Danny."

In your experience as part of the caring community,

have you noticed yourself falling into this pattern of strong initial support that dwindles as the days go by? If so, try this exercise. The next time you visit a friend or family in need, discipline yourself to set a time for a follow-up visit or call. This will help you resist the tendency to pay a great deal of attention initially and then taper off. And having a specific time to look forward to can be an extra encouragement to your friends. It might also be helpful to write their names on your calendar as a reminder to pray for them and to continue to keep in touch.

In some instances communication is strained or contact cut off because the individual or family does not welcome the caring gestures of others. Dale and Dan, on the other hand, wisely took the initiative to stay in touch with supportive friends. For almost two years Dan took over the youth minister's job at church, which allowed them to stay involved with many of Danny's friends. They also took a few trips as a family in the months after Danny's death. And they took constructive measures to compensate for the fatigue and irritability they experienced so that others would not be pushed away.

"Dale and I realized that we could not handle as much pressure as before. We had to cut back on some of our responsibilities and commitments. We were reminded that first comes our relationship with God, then our relationship to each other and our family. After those needs are met, then comes everything else," Dan comments. And Dale adds, "I knew that I was getting upset faster than normal. I could not handle as much stress and conflict as before. I am a cheerful person by nature, and I tried to focus on all the wonderful people in my life—especially my husband and children. They needed me to recover."

By taking into consideration their own physical,

emotional, and social needs, the Mills family was able to make adjustments that restored a sense of balance to life and nurtured closeness in relationships. They did not pull away from others or swing to the opposite extreme of depending upon others in a draining way.

Dan and Dale feel they were able to maintain this balance because they drew inner strength from their spiritual lives. "We rejuvenated our prayer life as a couple, literally clinging to God's promises. The main support came from special Scriptures we received from God within the first few weeks. There seemed to be more than one hundred verses that we had underlined in our Bibles over the year before Danny died that just jumped off the pages as we read God's Word. People's words would help, but God's special verses really put healing oil on our individual hurts. The second most significant support came from the prayers of dear friends in our community and from around the world. The prayers of God's people truly lifted us up."

The Mills family also had several friends who had lost children and successfully made it through their trial. Those friends were there to talk to and to answer questions with unique understanding and empathy. Dan recalls, "It was very encouraging to be told by these parents that with God's help we *were* going to make it through this difficult time."

Although the Millses never had a formal *support group*, as we now use the expression, individuals who had encountered similar trials were in a special position to offer comfort. They acted on the principle expressed in 2 Corinthians: "What a wonderful God we have—he is the Father of our Lord Jesus Christ, the source of every mercy, and the one who so wonderfully comforts and strengthens us in our hardships and trials. And why does he do this? *So that when others are troubled, needing our sympathy and encouragement,*

113

we can pass on to them this same help and comfort God has given us. . . . [I]n our trouble God has comforted us—and this, too, to help you: to show you from our personal experience how God will tenderly comfort you when you undergo these same sufferings. He will give you the strength to endure" (2 Cor. 1:3–7 TLB, emphasis added).

Formal support groups can also be an effective means of providing follow-up for families and individuals. During our research, however, we ran across an attitude about support groups that interrupted healthy follow-up. Some people felt that those who referred them to a local support group or to a caring professional wanted to absolve themselves and others in the church or community of any responsibility for being personally involved or need to dirty their hands in the dark business of grief, suffering, guilt, or death. And some distressed individuals fell into an isolation trap by harboring the idea that "only the support group *really* understands" and withdrawing from other contact.

While support groups can be extremely helpful to people in pain, they are not meant to be the sole mechanism through which comfort is given. If someone you care about is going through adversity, follow up on your friendship even if understanding support is also available in a group setting or from a counselor. And if you are currently recovering from a traumatic event, beware of limiting relationships only to a select group or to professionals. It is in everyone's best interest when friends, family members, pastors, counselors, and doctors work together in extending follow-up care.

Many life situations are not resolved with time alone. Even though the hurts may have begun with a crisis, they may result in continuing trials—a family business goes bankrupt, an automobile accident leaves a child in a coma, divorce results in assuming the role of a single parent. People experiencing these trials need comfort and hope long after the initial crisis is past. The church and community need to be there for them.

Individualize Your Care

No two people respond to a crisis in the same way, on the same timetable, or with the same feelings. People usually polarize to two extremes. When a crisis hits, one group digs in the trenches, musters their resources, becomes more aggressive, and prepares to fight through the difficulties. The second group tends to detach and assume a defeated "what's the use, all is hopeless" manner, becoming more passive in their reactions. It is obvious that we cannot respond in the same way to individuals who differ so widely in their response.

So what should we say to hurting people? What can we do to help? When we asked individuals who had gone through a crisis to list supportive responses as well as offensive comments or actions, an interesting pattern developed. The list of helpful versus hurtful behavior is contradictory. To some degree, *the lists are the same.* The following examples will give you an idea of the views expressed:

Helpful	**Hurtful**
My friends were so thoughtful in bringing food and preparing meals; I didn't have the strength to concern myself with cooking.	People brought food when I could have cared less about eating. I couldn't think of food at a time like that.
It meant a lot to me when friends were will-	My friends stuck around when I just

ing to just be there for me, even if we didn't say or do anything.

wanted to be alone to sort things through.

People provided factual information that explained our son's disease and prospects for recovery.

While my husband lay dying, the doctor rattled on with cold, clinical facts about his disease.

Friends took me out and invited me to their homes to get my mind off things. Later, when I was hospitalized, they came by with funny cards or videos.

People were forever trying to cheer me up as if it wasn't appropriate to be sad when you find out you have cancer!

The humorous contrast between how people viewed similar gestures of care leads us to helpful insights about maintaining relationships. First, it is obvious that caring responses must be offered in the context of what the hurting individual perceives as supportive instead of what *we* think they should appreciate. There is no one-size-fits-all care package that will always be received well. The importance of really listening before speaking or acting cannot be overemphasized. We have to tailor our response to the person's felt needs.

A second principle that stands out is the supreme importance of timing. What may be comfortable at one point may be offensive at another time. Again we must be sensitive to the person's feelings and physical condition. Discern when it is best to speak and when to listen, when to act and when to step out of the way.

The third insight shared by people we have counseled or surveyed is that love really does cover a multitude of blunders. It was not so much the actual comment made that mattered but who said it and how it was communicated. When it was clear that friends really cared, their presence and gestures of loving concern were appreciated—even if the words did not come out right or the help missed the mark.

You can use the following practical advice to improve your ability to say the right things. When you talk with a friend or family member during a difficult time, it is important to actively listen not only to the speaker's message but also to the feelings underlying the words. The feelings are as important as the facts. Here are some common mistakes that hinder our ability to actively listen and offer a meaningful caring response. Check the ones you may have inadvertently made.

Making Assumptions and Jumping to Conclusions

Don't assume you know how the person is feeling or why she is acting in a certain way. It is unwise to jump to conclusions based on circumstances you assume to be true or blame people you assume to be at fault. In his counseling, Dr. Fowler has discovered that the problem voiced initially is often *not* the real issue.

Cherry came to him complaining that her husband was financially irresponsible. After several sessions, however, it became apparent that her initial statements camouflaged deeper family problems. Since she only felt comfortable talking about her financial woes at first, this is where they started. Making assumptions based on surface level conversations with others can often lead us to faulty conclusions.

Even if the person asks a question, don't assume he is eager for advice or ready to act on it—people are often simply thinking out loud. For example, a single parent might ask, "Do you think I should go back to school?" Rather than responding quickly with your own opinion, it could be more helpful to ask, "Well, that depends. What do you think the advantages would be if you do?"

Giving Advice or Needing to Fix

"The inclination to give advice when someone is hurting comes from a sincere desire to help," writes psychologist Carol Travilla. "But it is not always 'help' that is helpful. Many times we endeavor to fix so that *we* will be more comfortable and not have to face the feelings of someone in pain.

"Suggestions are beneficial when the hurting person asks for them, but advice that sounds like a command intended to control the person or a demand usually results in defensiveness. To receive advice one must first feel understood and accepted. We are called to be *caregivers*, not *curegivers*."[2]

A Bible passage Dr. Fowler refers to frequently in his counseling is Galatians 6:2–5. In verse two we are told to "bear one another's burdens," yet verse five says, "each one shall bear his own load," meaning the work load and responsibilities expected of us. Before you step in to fix a problem or carry the weight of a decision, consider the difference between *burden* and *load*.

It is important to ask yourself before helping: "Is this a normal load that this person should be encouraged to handle by himself? Or is this a situation where there is an extra burden I need to help carry?" Constantly feeling the need to give advice, rescue, or take over for others may reflect an unhealthy need for control in your own life.

Being Judgmental or Critical

Especially during the vulnerable time of readjustment to a life-changing event, it is damaging to express disapproval of someone's conduct, even if the values reflected are glaringly different from ours. Criticism based upon our misguided notion that we always know what is best for everyone else will damage our relationships.

After the birth of her third child in four years, one young mother was frustrated about the limitations on her time and about her irregular attendance at a woman's group. She was struggling with the decision to give up membership in the group. "An older member told me I should be calling the ladies of the group to let them know I wouldn't be there," she recalls. "I felt like a little girl being scolded by my mother. I was infuriated because I didn't even have time to make the calls. I didn't need criticism—I needed help!"

Compassion, understanding, and acceptance are the main ingredients in strengthening relationships. People need the assurance that they are not alone in their struggles and pain. Pat answers and easy blanket solutions are seldom appreciated.

To emphasize the ineffectiveness of "I told you so" remarks, Dr. Fowler shares this story with his clients:

When my son was seven he was riding his bike down the street with his hands off the handlebars and fell off. He came into the house all skinned up and crying. I proceeded to tell him, "Chip, how many times have I told you not to ride a bike without hands on the handlebars?"

My preaching fell on deaf ears. Why? Because Chip was hurt and his mind was on finding ways to relieve the pain. So it is in relationships when a friend is hurting. Tender, loving care, not a critical or judgmental spirit, is in order. There may be an appropriate time later on when exhortation will be more effective. Often the experience itself is a great teacher without our added commentary!

Telling Your Own Story

It is very common for us to be engaged in a conversation that triggers memories of a similar experience. Suddenly we get sidetracked from active listening by the desire to do the talking. It usually happens something like this:

Jean: My sister just called—she miscarried her first child.

Lisa: Oh, my sister had a miscarriage too. But she got pregnant again right away. They just had a little boy this spring.

When the focus of the conversation shifts to *our* story, the hurting person may feel that the message she needed to convey was ignored or her feelings were discounted. Because distressed individuals want you to understand their particular situation, it is wise to avoid comments that minimize their loss or promote any sense of comparison. Even if your story has a happy ending, save it for *after* you have listened long enough to understand and acknowledge your friend's pain.

Those who seek to show sincere concern and put the hurting person at ease are able to assist others in a variety of creative, comfortable ways. As you act on the practical guidelines we've given for those who are part of the caring community, don't be held back by the fear that you will say or do the wrong thing. There is no one right thing to do. We simply need to remind ourselves to be patient and to individualize our care.

"Dan grieved a little differently than I did," Dale said. "He felt it helped to go to the cemetery, he watched videos of Danny, and he wanted to determine how the gun accident could have happened. I liked to talk about Danny but not about his death. We were able to respect these differences and remain sensitive to each other's needs. And our friends accepted our individual preferences."

Listening, caring, and sharing are the balance poles we can offer those who walk on the tightrope of stress. As Dan concluded, "We were supported and strengthened as we turned to God and as we allowed others to minister to us. We received strength from friends and family literally around the world. And, in turn, we've had the opportunity to reach out to others in our community during their time of need. We truly believe that *nothing* can happen to a Christian that God does not either plan or permit to happen."

Each individual will handle strong emotions differently, but we can learn from one another and improve our skills. In the next chapter we will look at more ways to maintain balanced, healthy support relationships.

9

The Safety Net

Support Through Interdependent Relationships

Before we leave the topic of the caring community, we would like to include the following excerpts from Diane's response to our survey. Diane, a young pastor's wife with expressive eyes and a quiet voice, wrote, "My husband Todd and I had three miscarriages. The last two were especially hard—they were six months apart. Todd and I grieve differently, so for a while I didn't think he was grieving. I didn't know if our parents, brothers, and sisters ever grieved, and that added to my hurt."

As Diane tells their family's story, look for the stress points we went over in the last chapter. Mentally review ways to avoid creating distance in your relationships by repeating the nonsupportive reactions. Also take note of constructive steps that would be of benefit to you in establishing a healthy, interdependent support network.

"We needed time to stop everything, but Todd's job doesn't allow that. Friends were understanding at first but then seemed to forget about it. I assumed they thought I should be over it. We appreciated it when friends took care of our two boys, brought in food, and sent notes within the first few days. These gestures helped immediately but eventually dropped off.

"As a constructive step, I went to counseling after my third loss. My counselor gave me positive things to work on each time. She listened as I poured out what was bottled up inside. And she helped me see that I was normal—not crazy for feeling that way. I also read lots of books. It helped me to understand and to know I wasn't alone. Todd gave constructive support too. He was and is always willing to listen and hold me when I cry.

"A parent of some of my students sent me a note immediately (she'd had a stillbirth) and later gave me a book to read. She sat with me and let me cry and cry on many different occasions. She has taken me to support groups and is always willing to listen. I've gained a new friend in her."

Diane also received nonsupportive comments from other individuals. When she listed them on our survey, she also noted her unspoken reaction next to each remark. Some of them are printed below as reminders to us all to be more understanding and gentle. Under each nonconstructive statement, we categorize the mistake it makes.

Hurtful Remarks	**Unspoken Reaction**
"There was something wrong; it must have been for the best." *(making unfounded assumptions)*	I still love them and miss them.
"You can have another baby in a few months." *(minimizing the loss)*	I need to grieve for these first. I have no hope left.
"Be thankful for the children you do have." *(telling her how she should feel)*	I know that! I don't need to be told.
"It's worse to lose a baby at eight months than at three months." *(insensitive comparison)*	And it's easier to lose a three-year-old than an eight-year-old? Ha!
Doctor: "There was nothing there." *(denial)*	Then why did you say I was pregnant, put me on prenatal vitamins, and set a due date!
"Shouldn't you be over this now? It's been a month." *(rushing the grieving process)*	A month! Who says grief ends in a month?

Evaluate your past conversations in light of the common mistakes and recommendations discussed here and in Chapter 8. Can you think of instances when any of the above communication problems created distance in your relationships? Are you prone to falling into one trap more often than others? If so, make a point of learning the skill of active listening, and watch your words more carefully. From now on, when you realize you're making one of these mistakes, bring your comment to a quick close and get back on track by asking a question focused on the other person.

BEARING ONE ANOTHER'S BURDENS

Have you ever wondered how much help and attention should be focused on a distressed individual? There are times when a mature person must depend almost entirely on another for support. And there are times when we are the ones called upon to offer help, comfort, and advice. How can we keep from tipping toward unhealthy dependency on those occasions? How can we recognize when we are hurting our relationships instead of helping? Here are some guidelines for discerning when and how much to help.

First, there should always be mutual respect and dignity, no condescending attitudes or ploys for control. Check the motive for giving help. When we come into mature adulthood, we assume a position of equality with other adults, treating one another as brothers and sisters in the Lord. God calls us to help bear one another's burdens—and to receive support—within the freedom of adult-to-adult interaction. The compassion of Christ and love for one another is our motivation.

Second, the help should restore a person to useful service and point them toward right living. Check the outcome of the support given. *Destructive patterns arise when help enables a person to become or to remain emotionally dependent, intellectually immature, or willfully irresponsible.* For example, parents may bail their child out of trouble, not letting the child learn from mistakes or suffer the consequences of disobedient behavior. A wife might cover for her alcoholic husband, enabling him to sin rather than confronting his destructive conduct. A caring friend may offer money and support to fix a problem that stems from a colleague's deliberate poor money management. In contrast true love will never be an accomplice to sin or selfishness.

Keith, a prosperous and big-hearted man with a soft spot toward his son, remarked, "My son has rarely kept a job for over a year. Whenever he ran low on funds he just called or wrote and I sent him money. But I'm coming to see that by allowing him to remain dependent upon me, I'm doing my son an injustice. I don't blame him—he's just a human taking the path of least resistance, like we all do. And I've been on the path of least resistance! But I'm determined to allow him the chance to establish himself."

That wasn't easy for Keith. After visiting his son's sparsely furnished college apartment, he almost gave in. "I came home and sat down in our room of fine leather furniture," Keith explained. "When I looked around at all we enjoyed and thought about his single lawn chair, tears came to my eyes. I called my wife and told her we had to get a trailer and load up some furniture for him right away. But she chuckled and kindly asked, 'Why? I went through college in a room decorated with orange crates!' "

Keith came to understand that love sometimes means withholding a helping hand.

True love will not rescue a person who always waits for others to make his choices. Healthy Christian compassion prompts us to serve others in ways that nurture their personal and spiritual growth—never in ways that ultimately are not in their best interest.

Adults should always be encouraged to assume the responsibilities of mature adulthood: to provide for themselves and their families, to work at productive tasks, to think through their convictions, and to act on honest and upright principles. In the daily concerns of life they should carry their own load. There should be a balance in the give-and-take of the relationship, with each person looking out for the interests of the other.

Remember the parable in Chapter 3 about David's journey to the land of mature adulthood? The story characterized healthy, interdependent living using the pronoun *we*. You do your part; I do mine. *We* pull together to make it through tough times.

COMPASSION BY CHOICE

When a person is overwhelmed by troubles and burdens and cannot help himself, we are called by Christ to step in and come to his aid. In contrast to fostering destructive dependence, acts of loving compassion help the other person get back on her feet. The story of the good Samaritan is a great example (Luke 10:30–37). The Samaritan felt compassion and love for the man who had been beaten by thieves and left to die on the roadside. Therefore he went to the injured man and bandaged his wounds, took him to an inn, and took care of him. The next day the Samaritan asked the innkeeper to look after him and paid for the care the distressed man needed. The Samaritan gave freely of his time and resources without expecting to be repaid.

Likewise we are instructed to care for the sick and broken-hearted, to seek justice for the oppressed, and to rescue the helpless. Proper compassion does not foster unhealthy dependency. And biblical compassion is not compulsive.

Because we each have limited resources—time, money, ability, and energy—it is necessary for us to exercise our power of choice. Our ministry to others in crisis cannot consume us to the point that the needs of our own families or our own needs are neglected for an extended period of time. That would indicate an imbalance that characterizes compulsive caregiving, not healthy service to those in need. We need to take a realistic approach and assess what we can and cannot do.

We can pray. We can be good listeners. We can alert others to a need and enlist their help on behalf of a distressed person. Yet we cannot do it all on our own. We cannot go without sleep or regular meals for extended periods of time. We cannot make everybody happy or solve the world's problems.

There will, of course, be times when we choose to temporarily live out of balance in order to help those we love. When the crisis at hand called for it, Jesus worked long hours, missed meals, and apparently had many short nights. Can you imagine His friends scolding Him for not taking care of Himself, or His rabbi pointing out His overcommitment? But Jesus chose to put the needs of others before His own. An occasionally erratic schedule, personal inconvenience, expense, and self-sacrifice will be required when we love people to the fullest as Jesus did.

Jesus also asked a man with physical handicaps, "Do you want to be made well?" (John 5:6) This is an appropriate question for those who feel most comfortable when they receive constant attention from others and for those addicted to the role of caregiver. If the relationships are to be healed, the dependent person must not only take the responsibility that comes with adult freedom but also he must begin to help himself. Having lived in the security of dependency, the individual may be afraid of making independent decisions, thinking for himself, and taking responsibility for his own emotions.

If you are indulging in overdependence on someone else, ask yourself honestly if you are willing to be healed. If so, list some constructive steps you can take to wean yourself from the other person's care and influence. Begin to do more for yourself, even when it seems easier to let someone else handle things. On the other hand, if you are currently carrying too much of someone else's load, gently back off the support until you are truly pulling together.

HOW TO EXPRESS AND RECEIVE HEALTHY SUPPORT

We all need one another. Yet we often have trouble knowing how to stay connected to a healthy support system. We aren't sure how to ask for help or how to give it, so we sometimes lean toward unhealthy independence by default. It often seems easier to withdraw or to avoid depending upon others.

Dr. Gary Chapman, who conducts national conferences on family life, has helped many people build their relationships by explaining these five ways in which individuals give and receive love. Understanding these languages of love can help you express support in ways that make the other person *feel* loved and accepted.

As you read through the list, number the ways we express and receive love from one to five in the order of their importance to you. For example, consider which expression makes you feel the most loved and label that category number one.

____ **Words.** We verbally express our love and concern in comments such as, "I'm sorry you're going through this," and in our willingness to talk about the trial. It is important to affirm and encourage one another.

____ **Acts of Service.** Acts of kindness and thoughtful gestures such as preparing food, caring for a child, providing transportation, making phone calls, or taking over some of the work load communicate love through practical help. As the Bible encourages, "let us not love in word or in tongue [only], but in deed and in truth" (1 John 3:18).

____ **Quality time.** Giving someone your time and undivided attention is another language of love. Many people feel loved not through something you do *for* them but by just being *with* them.

____ **Giving gifts.** A present is a universally accepted means of communicating that you care.

____ **Touch.** Sometimes a hug, an arm around the shoulder, or holding a hand communicates more clearly than words. Although physical demonstrations of affection are especially important for children, we never outgrow our need to be held.

We give and receive love in each of these ways, yet every individual has a primary love language. One of these ways of expressing love will be more meaningful, and will make the person *feel* most loved. Here's the catch: We may not be expressing our love in the person's primary love language and so our relationships suffer.

Do you see how the problems come up? A little boy gets very sick and his daddy buys him a new toy (love demonstrated through gift giving). But the child still doesn't *feel* loved if he really wanted a hug (love expressed through touch) or wanted to hear "I love you, and I'm sure sorry you don't feel good" (love communicated out loud). We need to know one another well enough to recognize and deliberately use the loved one's primary love language.

We need to study the things that please our children, mates, and friends. Not everyone understands love best in the way you prefer to give it. Healthy interdependence requires that a father meet his son's needs in ways that are meaningful to the son. We cannot allow our preferences to dictate the ways we reach out to others in their time of need. As emphasized in the last chapter, it is extremely important to individualize our care.

Not everyone, however, will be sensitive and understanding. For those on the receiving end of nonsupportive comments, Diane suggests, "Ignore the insensitive words of well-meaning people who don't understand. Love them, but don't dwell on their remarks. Get involved with a supportive group of people and keep talking."

Because of bad experiences in the past, some people are afraid to depend upon others or to openly suggest which expressions of love would be most appreciated. Even if you offer to help, they insist they can get along by themselves. If others have failed to support them in the past, their independence may be a self-protective reaction to having others hurt them, reject them, or manipulate them. The person may withdraw, saying in effect, "I don't need you; I'll be self-sufficient—then you can't hurt me anymore or desert me."

With sensitivity and with individualized efforts, these destructive patterns can be replaced by healthier behaviors. Caring friends who have gone through similar struggles can be of special help. "Because this has happened to me, I feel that God has used me in helping others in this situation," Diane explained. "I have a special tenderness and understanding toward these other women that I don't think I had before."

If you have the desire to comfort and encourage others but your emotions trip you up, read on. In the next chapter we will look more closely at how to handle the feelings that impair your ability to relate well to others.

10

When Emotions Trip You Up

How to Handle Emotional Overload

During the pregnancy with their youngest child, Evan, Rita and Arlan shared a running inside joke about what might happen this time to make the birth more eventful. There were no heart surgeries on the immediate horizon for Erin, and the other children were doing well. The delivery went smoothly, and when they checked out of the hospital Arlan teased that they finally "got one right."

But the day they brought the baby home Arlan was kicked in the knee by a one-thousand-pound heifer while he was loading cattle. It dropped him to the ground instantly. He limped in the house with a sheepish grin on his face. "It's always something!" he quipped, laughing off Rita's request that he see a doctor. Arlan propped his leg up and applied an ice bag for the remainder of the afternoon. But his knee continued to swell and the pain became intense.

Meanwhile Evan began showing signs of reacting to breast milk. This time they had suspected they might encounter the problem and had electrolyte water on hand just in case. Rita immediately stopped nursing and called the specialist to set up an appointment for the next morning. Evan could have nothing to eat, except electrolyte solution to prevent dehydration, for twenty-four hours. He cried almost constantly from digestional irritation and hunger.

By evening things had gotten pretty out of hand. Arlan and Rita had four kids under age five who needed attention. Rita couldn't lift them, and Arlan couldn't carry them. Neither parent felt up to climbing the stairs to the children's bedrooms to put them to sleep. At one point all four kids were crying. The situation looked so ridiculous Arlan and Rita didn't know whether to laugh or join in!

Fortunately Arlan's folks stopped by to see how things were going. They kindly took over and got the kids ready for bed. The next morning Rita and Arlan headed to the local emergency room to get an X ray, crutches, and pain pills for Arlan before heading to the Omaha hospital with Evan. Evan was immediately admitted, and Arlan decided it would be best if he stayed with the baby since he couldn't walk anyway. Rita went home to take care of the other children.

As this story points out, it is not always a single life-disturbing event that causes emotional overload. Often it is the cumulative effect of a series of events. It is like loading brick after brick on the back of the camel then topping it off with the infamous straw! Even minor changes in life patterns are stressful. And major changes produce enormous anxiety and tension—even if they are positive changes. Relationships can easily become strained under the pressure. So how can you lighten your load if stress is inevitable during life's tough times?

First, don't take on additional loads unless they are unavoidable. Start unloading self-imposed bricks; reduce stress every chance you get. Second, learn healthy techniques of stress management. Third, think ahead and avoid the straw—it could be the pressure to meet a deadline, an attitude of ingratitude from those you help, or getting a cold. In this chapter you will find practical ways to handle emotional overload.

UNLOADING EXTRA WEIGHT

It almost goes without saying that certain behaviors will *always* damage your relationships. Yet it is essential to know these basics. You may already know many of the following suggestions, but you may not be implementing them. Bear with us as we repeat the obvious.

Avoid Secrets, Lies, or Cover-ups

Dick and Tammy Wilkinson were enjoying the delights of fast lane living until it all came to a sudden halt when Dick suffered a massive heart attack at age 43. Tammy knew, four days before Dick was informed, that his only hope for survival would be a heart transplant. "Keeping it secret didn't change the facts; he had to know eventually. But it began to drive a wedge between us."

Open, honest communication is the most constructive response, even when the truth is painful. Since Dick's heart failure and lengthy recovery, Tammy and Dick have learned not to lie or pretend everything's OK—even to protect each other. Getting things out in the open allows you to share the experience and support one another through it. Withholding information or feelings creates emotional distance in the relationship.

Lying about an affair will not make it go away. Covering up a drug or alcohol addiction will not strengthen your family. Instructing children to act as if nothing is wrong when there is abuse or marital tension in the home destroys trust.

These examples are extreme. But even petty phoniness or dishonesty will contribute to emotional overload and weaken relationships. Expect interpersonal problems if you sidestep straightforward communication and resort to scheming, manipulation, exaggerated pleading, or conniving. Instead, create an open environment for sharing information, feelings, and requests.

Are there any areas where you and your spouse, child, or close friend are being less than honest with one another? Are there unhealthy secrets straining your relationship? If these questions prick your conscience, you must find the courage to break the cycle of deception for the sake of the relationships you cherish.

Watch Out for Extremes

Stress drives people to extremes. In times of crisis we often see an accentuation of personality traits. The person who was a hard worker tends to be driven to work all the harder. The procrastinator may delay even more. The shy person may be more withdrawn while an impatient person can become more restless, irritable, and short-tempered. And so it goes.

As one therapist phrased it, when we are under intense stress we "act more like ourselves than ever." We tend to fall back on our old ways of handling problems and take the reactions to the extreme. This isn't necessarily a problem. But if the cycle is left unchecked, addictions and compulsions may develop, and preexisting problems may become more severe.

Don't be fooled into focusing only on the disturbing behavior—it may be merely a side effect of stress. You may stop biting your fingernails, interrupting others in conversation, or doing whatever behavior you dislike, only to find another excessive behavior cropping up somewhere else. It's like mowing dandelions. Being aware of your tendencies toward extremes during times of stress, however, can help you manage your emotional overload. Here is an easy-to-remember rule of thumb: *Under stress, avoid excess.*

Lift Off the Load of Guilt and Shame

Teresa, a young, recently divorced mother of two preschoolers, commented, "I think I could handle my emotions if I didn't have to deal with my responsibilities at the same time. But I feel so driven to get everything done, and there's no one else to do it. And sometimes I get carried away. I used to be a pretty good housekeeper. Now I'm compulsive about wanting everything in place. My life is a mess but at least my house is in order—even the closets!"

Teresa was carrying a crushing load of constant guilt when she came to see Dr. Fowler for counseling. Because Teresa's mother felt a dysfunctional need to control, she attempted to make Teresa feel guilty for decisions Teresa made after her divorce. At the clinic Teresa was taught to screen out invalid input and to counter her increasing depression by reminding herself of the truth: *Just because Mother doesn't approve of what I choose doesn't make it foolish. I don't need to feel guilty or apologize for making my own decisions and doing what I feel is best for myself and the children.*

False guilt frequently entangles itself in our responses to difficulties. Unlike true guilt associated with specific offenses we can confess to God, this imaginary guilt is often characterized by a continual *I am to blame for everything that goes wrong* feeling and a vague sense of shame.

Paul Tournier, a noted Christian physician and author from Switzerland, distinguished between true and false guilt this way: "A feeling of 'functional [false] guilt' is one which results from social suggestion, fear of taboos, or of losing the love of others. A feeling of 'value [true] guilt' is the genuine consciousness of having betrayed an authentic standard; it is a free judgment of the self by the self. . . . 'False guilt' is that which comes as a result of the judgments and suggestions of men. 'True guilt' is that which results from divine judgment. . . . Therefore *real guilt is often something quite different from that which constantly weights us down, because of our fear of social judgment and the disapproval of men.* We become independent of them in proportion as we depend on God" (emphasis added).[1]

The good news is we can lift off the unbearable emotional load of guilt and shame. True guilt can be cleansed through sincere confession before God when we ask and receive His forgiveness. If we are honestly in the wrong, we need to apologize and if necessary make restitution to people we have offended. False guilt must be recognized for what it is and dislodged by truth.

How much guilt are you carrying?

In *We Are Driven*, Dr. Robert Hemfelt, Dr. Frank Minirth, and Dr. Paul Meier describe statements which are typical of guilt-ridden people.[2] If you check two or more of the remarks listed below, you are carrying excessive guilt:

____ *"I have a tendency to 'awfulize' situations. Gloom and doom are my specialty. I can out-worry anybody."*

____ *"I apologize too often. I misread people's reactions to me and fear that I have angered or disappointed them. 'I'm sorry' is one of my favorite phrases. 'It's all my fault' is another."*

____ *"I don't know how to respond to a compliment. Rather than say 'thank you' when I am complimented, I usually try to invalidate the nice words by mentioning one of my shortcomings."*

____ *"I feel fragmented. Because I overcommit myself by saying yes too often, I feel pulled in a dozen directions. The positive part of my overcommitment is that I'm so busy I don't have time to dwell on my guilt."*

____ *"I worry that God is keeping score. Whereas some people count on God to love and to forgive them no matter what, I imagine God is planning appropriate punishment for all my wrongs."*

____ *"I feel that I constantly have to justify my right to exist, and no matter how much I've done, I feel inadequate. I'm not sure I deserve to exist, but I'm certain I don't deserve lasting happiness."*

Accept the Loss

In the aftermath of her divorce, Teresa not only needed to lift off her guilt, she also needed to sort through and relinquish many dreams. This is easier when the wound is clean, as when Rita's father was killed in an accident. Rita had enjoyed a close, healthy relationship with her dad, so she was spared the pain of guilt and regret. Yet long after she had worked through her grief and had come to accept his death, Rita experienced bouts of intense sadness. Her wedding day when her father could not walk her down the aisle, the birth of her children, holidays, and other events triggered wistful sorrow. It was natural for her to wish that things had been different.

It is much harder when the wounds fester with the thought, *If only he would change, my dream could come true.* As a teenager, Teresa dreamed of marrying a man who would love and protect her and be a model father to her children. But soon after her wedding, her husband's deep personal problems, coupled with her own insecurities, destroyed her budding dreams like an early frost. Financial setbacks accentuated the problems. Now Teresa struggled with aching disappointment. "I know I have to let go of my expectation that he will ever be what I hoped for and love him as he is, but dreams die hard. Even though the divorce is final, part of me still clings to that shred of hope that he will come back and things will be better."

Teresa is not the only person who lives with the feeling that life has let them down. We would all like to see things different from what they are in some respects, but we've got to move on in life. We can lighten our emotional load by letting go of lost dreams and accepting what we cannot change.

STRESS MANAGEMENT TECHNIQUES

Your relationships will be influenced not only by stressful events but also by your response to them. Here are some common sense suggestions for stress management.

Keep Life in Perspective

During counseling it was determined that much of Teresa's depression was coming from repressed anger. Teresa was encouraged to begin to monitor her thinking. Dr. Fowler explains, "If you take a pair of binoculars and look through them the normal way, you will enlarge the object you're looking at. That's the way many of us see negative events. Magnified. But then we flip the binoculars around and see all the good things reduced to insignificant size. The lens we're looking through distorts our perspective—exaggerating negatives and minimizing positives. It's important that we look at all of life through the same lens. The ability to see something positive in a bad situation gives us hope."

The importance of this outlook is summed up in a poster:

> *Roses have thorns or*
> *Thorns have roses.*
> *How do you see life?*

Learn to Think More Positively

If you recognize that your outlook is often negative but you can't locate the thinking process causing the problem, we can help you in your search. Imagine for a moment that you are a participant in one of our workshops on healthy stress management. As we describe the common types of distorted thinking, take a pencil and put a check mark next to the ones that might apply in your life. Some items may overlap.

____ *All-or-nothing thinking.* A person sees things in black-and-white categories. If she falls short of being perfect, she perceives herself as a complete failure. She feels she must do everything or nothing; things are all good or all bad.

____ *Overgeneralization.* One sees a single negative experience as a never-ending pattern of defeat. One memory lapse, for example, may lead to the conclusion, "This will happen over and over again."

____ *Mental filter.* Here an individual picks out a single negative detail and dwells on it exclusively, thus viewing the whole situation as negative. This thinking is analogous to using a drop of ink to discolor the entire beaker of water; the person's vision of reality becomes darkened.

____ *Disqualifying the positive.* In this instance the person rejects positive experiences by insisting that "they don't count" for some reason or another. He maintains a negative attitude even though his everyday experiences may contradict it. Ten good things and one frustration add up to a horrible day!

____ *Jumping to conclusions.* The individual arbitrarily jumps to a negative conclusion without definite facts to support her opinion. She will worry at the slightest hint of a problem, assuming a negative outcome before anything bad happens.

____ *Self-fulfilling prophecy.* The person lives up to a negative expectation from someone else like "You'll never amount to anything." Or he anticipates that things will turn out badly and is convinced that his own prediction is an already-established outcome. Perhaps he thinks, "It's no use, I'm going to die." As unrealistic as the thought may be, the person is convinced it is true. He may work against his chance of recovery by refusing to cooperate with treatment or by losing hope.

____ *Emotional reasoning.* This distortion leads one to take her emotional reactions as evidence of the truth: "I feel overwhelmed at the thought of balancing our finances; therefore it is impossible to learn." This kind of reasoning is misleading because feelings often distort rational thoughts.

____ *Should statements.* Here the individual tries to motivate himself by saying, "I should do this," or "I must do that." Paradoxically, these statements often cause him to feel pressured and resentful, leading to apathy and a lack of motivation.

____ *Labeling or mislabeling.* Personal labeling is an extreme form of overgeneralization that results in a completely negative outlook or self-image. Instead of describing her error, she may attach a negative label to herself: "I'm lousy." Sentences that begin with "I'm a . . ." are clues to her problem.

____ *Assuming personal responsibility.* This distortion, which is the mother of false guilt, involves assuming responsibility for a negative event when there is no basis for doing so.

____ *Attention seeking.* A person may assume a negative or depressed outlook to draw sympathy and support from others. He seeks attention through a "poor me" outlook.

Locating the source of your negative perspective is the first step in moving toward a more cheerful, hopeful attitude. The next step is to combat negative thoughts head-on. How is this done? By actively changing the way you talk to yourself.

Tell Yourself the Truth

We can learn how to replace our old, negative, fear-inducing thought patterns with new programming. Here are some examples of negative inner dialogue:

- "It's just no use! There's no way out."
- "I can't handle this."
- "Things never work out for me."
- "If only I had (more money, a better marriage, a close friend, someone to take care of me), then I could feel secure."
- "I just can't take it anymore!"

By contrast, truth talk is positive, specific, present tense dialogue with yourself. For example, when you are anxious about a coming event, tell yourself affirming truths such as:

- "I can have ups and downs and still be emotionally healthy. It's OK to have feelings, and the fact that I recognize and monitor them is a good sign."
- "Even though I'd like to avoid this situation, I

will not. I choose to go ahead, accept the unpleasant feelings, and do what I think is best. I may not like it, but I can get through it; God will give me the strength I need to handle all things."

The truth cuts through the deceptions and distorted perceptions. For a more complete discussion on how to change your inner messages, we suggest you read Dr. Chris Thurman's book, *The Lies We Believe.* It is vitally important to renew your mind through reading Scripture and to control your thoughts. As the ancient philosopher Epictetus wrote, "Man is disturbed not by things but by the view he takes of them."

Learn to Relax

Because of Teresa's need to please everyone and handle her work load at home and work, she became frantically activistic. To lighten her emotional load, she needed to give herself permission to relax and to learn some effective ways to unwind.

When we encounter crisis situations, our adrenaline level rises, our hearts jump into our throats, and we often experience a tightness in the chest or neck. While this is a typical, spontaneous response to bad news, it is not desirable as a long-term condition. It is difficult to relate to people when you are tense or nervous. Don't fall into a life-style of perpetual anxiety.

Here are some relaxation exercises Dr. Fowler asks his patients to do when they are keyed up. Try this breathing exercise first then work through the muscle relaxation exercise.

Breathing Exercise

A. Sit in a chair or lie down in a quiet area.

B. Take a deep breath and hold it, counting as long as you can—1,001 . . . 1,002 . . . 1,003 . . .

C. When you feel you are about to burst, let the air out of your lungs slowly.

D. After all the air is out, breathe deeply—don't allow yourself to gasp for air.

E. Take several slow deep breaths and then hold your breath again, repeating the counting process. If you are beginning to relax, you will be able to count to a higher number. (Your body needs more oxygen when under stress, so when you're relaxed there is less need for oxygen and you should be able to increase the count.)

Muscle Relaxation

Muscle relaxation exercises are similar to the natural body response that often accompanies a yawn. Specific muscles contract and tense up, then release and relax.

To begin, settle back as comfortably as you can. Let all your muscles go loose and heavy. Wrinkle up your forehead . . . wrinkle it tighter . . . then stop wrinkling your forehead . . . relax and smooth it out. Now tense up your right shoulder . . . contract the muscles even tighter . . . now relax.

Starting at the top of your body and working your way down, continue to isolate different muscle groups. Follow the same process of tensing and relaxing each one. Try to achieve deeper and deeper levels of relaxation.

Any time you feel anxious and worried, you can use these relaxation techniques to help control your feelings and their physical signs (such as sweating, higher pulse, or tightening in the chest). When those tensions occur, take time to break the pressure cycle. Push back and breathe deeply or get up and walk around for a few minutes.

144

Better yet, set aside a few minutes every day for relaxation exercises. A complete series of tension-reducing exercises set to calming music is available on "Quiescence" (Nashville: Thomas Nelson, 1991), an instructional video by Jeri Perchinski, a licensed occupational therapist at the Minirth-Meier Clinic.

If you need help unwinding, you might also find it relaxing and therapeutic to work with your hands, complete routine chores, or listen to restful music. It's not by accident that people say "peace and quiet" in the same breath. Noise and confusion contribute to stress, so if at all possible, schedule periods of quiet and solitude in your day.

A Place for Tears

In addition to exercise, tears are one of the natural release valves God designed into our system. Although our society has implied that tears are a sign of weakness or immaturity, such is not always the case. Tears speak eloquently when you have no words to express the intense tenderness, compassion, or sorrow you feel for someone. When you are overwhelmed with feelings of despair, hopelessness, sadness, or even joy and relief that words cannot describe, tears convey the depth of your feeling. At such times crying can release bottled-up feelings and help restore emotional equilibrium.

Take One Day at a Time

Fear of the future or pain from the past can drain the emotional strength you need for relationships today. We cannot live in the past; we can only learn from it. No one can go back and rewrite history or erase a tragic event. It is vital to accept that the past cannot be changed. God can, however, change the impact of the past on your present relationships if you allow Him to work in your life. Don't use past pain as an excuse

145

for present fears. *The past can certainly explain some of our fears but never excuse them.*

Ease the fear of something you dread in the future by focusing on one day at a time. Fight the overwhelming anxiety of "what if" with "what is." Acknowledge to yourself that you are afraid, then remind yourself, "Yes, it would be bad if that happened; it's OK to feel afraid. But it hasn't happened yet. If it does happen, I'll deal with it then. In the meantime I need to direct my emotional energy and efforts toward the situation I face today."

When you feel the urge to worry, try to practice what Hewlett-Packard CEO John Young calls "just-in-time worrying." As he says, "If you worry too soon, things will change in the interim, so you end up having to deal with them twice."[3] This approach fits with the biblical instruction, "Do not worry about tomorrow, for tomorrow will worry about its own things. Sufficient for the day is its own trouble" (Matt. 6:34).

Face Your Fears

Excessive worry is only one expression of destructive fear. We all live with many fears; some are healthy signs of adjustment, and others can jeopardize our relationships. As Dr. Fowler warns his clients, "Fear seems to be the single common denominator which can push a painful experience into the realm of the unbearable."

Fear often disguises itself as anger. People can become defensive and irritated when they feel afraid. Therefore, when friction in relationships increases, or when you find yourself overreacting to a situation, it is wise to consider whether any of the following common fears are prompting insecurity. Be honest as you consider whether any of these fears are undermining your relationships.

These are sensitive areas where you may feel vulnerable. You might find it easier to admit to the first portion of the statement than the underlying fear, but do not dismiss the fear too quickly. Check any statements that apply:

____ *"I'm a private person and rarely volunteer to assume responsibility in a group. (I dread making public mistakes.)"*

____ *"I'm eager to please; I hate letting people down. I always want to get a good evaluation from my friends and family. (I worry about upsetting or disappointing someone and losing their approval.)"*

____ *"I avoid conflict at all costs and tend to be overprotective of time together in close friendships. (I fear rejection or loss of love and closeness.)"*

____ *"I don't like to talk about death or growing older. I avoid conversations about meeting God face-to-face. (I'm anxious about the possibility of death or God's judgment.)"*

____ *"I'm not a risk taker; I don't like facing new situations. And I rarely travel. (I fear the unknown or unfamiliar.)"*

____ *"I hate feelings of helplessness; I prefer to be in charge of things. (I'm afraid of losing control.)"*

____ *"I would classify myself as a perfectionist. I like excellent work and achievement. (I'm afraid to fail.)"*

____ *"I tend to be a loner. I don't like to get too close to or share my feelings with others. I have a hard time saying, 'I love you.' (I fear intimacy.)"*

____ *"After experiencing a bad relationship, it's hard for me to seek out others to befriend. I don't view many people as loyal or faithful friends. (I fear being abandoned or betrayed.)"*

____ *"I find myself always taking over-the-counter drugs and wouldn't think of taking a trip without them. I hate going out in bad weather. And I tend to avoid competi-*

147

tive sports and active leisure activities. (I fear being sick or hurt.)"

A good way to calm your fears is to meditate on Scripture. Choose Bible verses that relate to your specific fear. You can begin with these passages:

Fear of Intimacy
Colossians 3:9–13
1 Thessalonians 3:12
1 John 4:16–21

Fear of the Unknown
Psalm 121
1 John 5:4
Psalm 23

Fear of Being out of Control
Proverbs 3:5–6
Psalm 119:9–11
Philippians 4:6–9

Fear of Failure
Matthew 11:28–30
2 Timothy 1:9
James 1:5

Fear of Rejection or Abandonment
John 6:37
Matthew 6:31–33
2 Timothy 2:13

Fear of Being Hurt
Matthew 5:7
James 5:11
James 1:2–4

Reprogram Your Fears

Focus on one reading for 15 to 30 minutes as you complete this exercise. Read the passage and meditate on how it can address your anxiety. Write out key phrases or insights, memorize them, and read them to yourself every morning. Your behavior will move in the direction of your repeated thoughts. Interrupt the thoughts that are feeding your fears whenever they occur and replace those messages with positive, truthful statements.

Verbalizing your fears can also help take away their sting.

Bond with Others

Talking with a close friend at least once a week about your struggles can also be an effective way to handle the emotional overload of a crisis. Bonding is a key to emotional health. Even if you feel like withdrawing after the initial problems are past, you will benefit from staying connected with others.

Take the initiative to stay in touch. Remind each other that serious problems are seldom handled once and for all. Instead, the emotions will linger and affect your life long into the future. Although you will probably do most of the talking at first, as time goes on it is important for you to *listen*—and take action based on your friend's advice when you know it is best. Don't turn the sessions into monologues that feed your needs for attention and support but do little else, or you may wear thin your friendship. If you keep the relationship on an adult-to-adult level, not allowing the sharing to breed the dependency of a parent-to-child interaction, your friendship should be one of growth and satisfaction for both of you.

As mentioned earlier, many people find that keeping a spiritual journal is immensely helpful for working through emotional issues they feel uncomfortable sharing with others.

STRESS PREVENTION

Nothing mentioned above implies that you should not attempt to change your circumstances where it's appropriate. We encourage you to do anything you can today to prevent or at least to prepare for stressful events. Take practical precautions to avoid setting youself up. If you fear cancer, get a complete checkup, eat right, and exercise. If you fear getting laid off at work, set aside some savings and sharpen your skills to cushion the blow if it occurs.

Plan ahead. You can't control everything that might happen, but many factors governing your response are under your influence. Choose to structure your environment to bring out the best in yourself and others— cut back your schedule, for example. Rely on routine. As Dr. Shad Helmstetter, author of *Choices*, wrote, "It is only when you exercise your right to *choose* that you can also exercise your right to *change*."[4] Here are other ways you can change your relationships for the better by maintaining emotional balance.

Sleep and Regular Exercise

The late Vince Lombardi once said, "I think good physical conditioning is essential. . . . A man who is physically fit performs better at any job. Fatigue makes cowards of us all." It seems insensitive to suggest that many relationships could be improved by simply getting enough sleep and regular exercise, but in general, tired people are hard to get along with!

Doctors agree that adults need from eight to ten hours sleep a night. Avoid sleep deprivation or the excessive sleep indicative of depression. Dreaming is an essential psychological release valve for letting off emotional pressure. Therefore, getting a proper amount of sleep really is the first practical step for preventing emotional overload.

Exercise is perhaps the most effective means to relieve stress and lower adrenaline levels. Exercise helps clean out your system, promotes relaxation, and builds up your serotonin level. Interestingly, research among AIDS patients found that the one thing that often put AIDS into remission was exercise. Encouraging people to exercise is not new advice.

But suppose your business is near bankruptcy, like

Dr. Fowler's client Carl, and you have time to manage little more than aerobic swivels in your office chair. Then what? While we would recommend twenty to thirty minutes of aerobic exercise at least three times a week, it is not an all-or-nothing benefit package. Walking or any increase in physical activity can help. Carl began parking farther from his office and walked, took the stairs instead of the elevator, and took a brisk walk around the block during his lunch hour. Improvise. Learn to look for opportunities to be active.

Seek Positive Outlets for Emotional Expression

The fine arts provide a natural outlet for emotion. Writing poetry, songs, or stories can be an effective means of expression. Listening to soothing music or reading inspirational material can also help you unwind. Teresa found that listening to upbeat music when she felt depressed lifted her spirits. And relaxing music calmed her soul when she felt tense. In fact, changing her radio station turned out to be a quick and easy way to adjust her attitudes and to help control her mood swings.

After a devastating loss, a person who has been deeply hurt may pour himself into fighting for a specific cause. A man whose son died of cystic fibrosis, for instance, may choose to use his business expertise to head a fund-raising drive for research. Or a bereaved mother may devote herself to the efforts of Mothers Against Drunk Driving. In cases such as these, social activism may give outlet to overwhelming emotion.

Watch Your Diet

Certain vitamin and nutritional changes can influence your body's ability to manage a crisis. For example, vitamin B^6, magnesium, and potassium supplements are sometimes recommended. And extreme highs or lows in sugar levels are discouraged. In some cases your physician may feel prescriptions for certain medications would be helpful. Although this subject lies outside the scope of this book, we would encourage you to *seek professional advice* before turning to any prescription or nonprescription drug for relief. Specifically, stay away from potentially addictive substances such as alcohol, marijuana, tranquilizers, stimulants, or anti-depressants.

Are You Doing It?

Here is a random listing of ways to handle stress that were mentioned in this chapter. Give yourself a point for each one you are already doing. Congratulate yourself if you scored ten or more points. Circle items you want to incorporate into your life in the future. Then choose two areas to work on this week.

__ accept what you cannot change

__ have regular times of prayer

__ talk with a trusted friend

__ laugh

__ cast off false guilt

__ meditate on Scripture

__ learn to relax more often

__ keep a journal

__ monitor your thinking

__ eat balanced meals

__ avoid distorted perceptions

__ write things out

__ control adrenaline surges

__ get proper sleep

__ allow tears to flow

__ listen to soothing music

__ let go of lost dreams

__ exercise

Humor Yourself

Last, here's something fun you can do to lighten your emotional load. Get with friends and have a good laugh! Laughter can reduce tension and stress. Humor helps communicate ideas and opinions and is also effective as a means to reduce quarreling. A willingness to see the silly side of things can put others at ease, lessen anxiety, and help you cope.

Hans Selye, a medical researcher and neuroendocrinologist at the University of Montreal, conducted studies on stress that showed how the body could manufacture its own poisons when under siege by negative emotions.[5] Conversely, pioneering research by Norman Cousins at University of California at Los Angeles shows mounting scientific evidence that hope, faith, love, purpose, and laughter are powerful biochemical prescriptions for combating illness and restoring health.[6] Laughter is good medicine for the soul.

Studies have also shown that excessive TV viewing promotes depression. So if you must pass time in a hospital room, do as Erin, Rita, and Arlan did—opt for cartoons and funny videos. Or read jokes from *Reader's Digest* or the *Saturday Evening Post* magazines. Caution: football bloopers, Bill Cosby, and Disney cartoons can be habit-forming!

Part II of this book will integrate many of the ideas we have covered thus far and offer suggestions for those who would like to improve their relationships through specific tough times—changing residence, facing critical illness, widowhood, divorce, or financial setbacks. In the next few pages you will meet some interesting people and learn principles that apply regardless of the stressful circumstances you face.

We will begin by looking at the very common stress of moving to a new community.

Part II
Restoring
Balance After . . .

11

Moving

"I picked up and packed every last belonging and left sunny southern California for the dream Mary Tyler Moore TV job in Minneapolis," Kay begins. "As a single adult, of course, I moved to Minneapolis alone. I hadn't anticipated, however, the loss of my support system of family and friends or the physical and emotional stress of the move. I left a safe job surrounded by friends and had no idea how severe the adjustment would be. High expectations, plus an inability to find a support network and express my needs, set me up for huge disappointment."

Kay was only one of countless individuals who have felt uprooted, lonely, and let down after moving to a new community. According to the *Reader's Digest Guide to Moving*, the average American moves more than ten times. In a single year alone more than forty million of us—roughly one in six families—will change addresses, and it will cost us more than $5 billion. Relocating family and possessions may be one of the most difficult things we will ever do.

In addition to the financial considerations of moving,

this emotionally stressful experience often includes a shift in employment, friendships, place of residence, and proximity to extended family members. Even when the move is a beneficial change, it still causes a strain on relationships.

But the stress and confusion of moving can be minimized with smart planning and preparation. And the emotional impact of moving can be eased if you accept it as normal and reach out to acquire new friends. Moving can stimulate personal growth, make us adaptable, give us the opportunity to enjoy new experiences, and broaden our scope of understanding. Here are some areas to help make your move a positive change.

Take the Initiative to Establish New Friendships

Dr. Fowler was a college professor for a number of years before accepting his current position as the director of clinical services for the Minirth-Meier Clinic. Although the move was a positive one, there were common adjustments to be made.

"When I walked across campus everybody knew me," Rick remembers. "Our neighborhood was small and friendly. At church I taught classes, and people sought out my counsel. When we moved I was stripped of old roles and identity. I had to prove myself to many people when I assumed my new position."

The Fowlers decided to join a larger church whose congregation included many professors and students from a well-known seminary in the area. Rick was suddenly feeling like a pretty small fish in a much larger pond than the one he was accustomed to. Even at church, he felt as if he was expected to prove himself again. Because Rick was traveling more, it became harder for him and his wife to establish close new relationships with other couples. To complicate matters, their new church was not close to home, and many people lived much farther away. Just navigating the unfamiliar expressways hampered getting to know people.

For years the Fowlers had enjoyed get-togethers with close friends. Now they suddenly felt adrift and alone, unable to get past superficial smiles and greetings. Rick would like to be able to say that they took the initiative, boldly inviting folks over and coming to church eager to make new friends. Yet their frame of mind and his travel obligations really hindered them. Slowly, however, they did make new friendships that have become just as special as their old ones.

The Fowler children, too, felt the displacement and uncertainty. Their daughter especially struggled with letting go of the past where she had felt emotionally safe. She was in the eighth grade at the time of their move, and she found it necessary to mourn the loss of her old home and friends. Her grieving process was very similar to accepting the death of a loved one.

The Fowlers's first year was not easy. But looking back, they see that it was a year of great growth spiritually and emotionally. As their supporting props were removed, they learned to trust God more and to appreciate one another.

In the same way, the lack of outside friendships following a move can have the benefit of drawing any family closer as they lean on one another. Establishing traditions that move with you and doing things together as a family will help you feel at home no matter where you live. No husband or wife or child can be the sole provider for another's relational needs however. And close friendships are especially important for single adults who cannot turn to their immediate family for encouragement and support.

Kay had a difficult time reestablishing a network of friends. She recalls, "My work load was so heavy at the TV station that I hardly saw the people I lived with. I remained very isolated for the most part. The world saw my professional act, and even in private it was hard to express my real pain. I was not honest with my feelings of huge disappointment in this dream job, my anger at God for leading me up there, and my extreme anger toward a very controlling boss. My lifelong habit of denying anger at all costs created this pressure cooker inside me that kept me alone and unreal around other people."

Keep in Touch with Old Friends

Keeping in contact with friends left behind can be a lifeline of support during the cycle of readjustment, as Kay recalls: "My phone bills were outrageous. I remember locking myself in a video editing room one day at work and calling a friend in California for support— just someone to say 'I care.' In the dead of winter I received flowers from an old friend in Santa Monica. I would recommend to everyone who moves that they keep at least one long-distance friend who knows them well enough to remain a steady anchor through the changes. During my most recent job change back to California, I needed to call my closest friends in New Jersey and Nebraska. But after four months or so, my long-distance calls were not as necessary. Now I write —things are not as urgent, and I have supportive friends here too."

We all prefer to be involved in some relationships that give us security, but moving assumes dropping or reshaping many of those relationships to various degrees. Shifting friendships is a delicate process, and it's best to avoid abrupt shifts. Don't avoid saying goodbye but resist the temptation to sever all ties with old friends. Gently moving a family from one circle of friends to another is like handing a newborn from one person to another; the first set of arms continues to hold the baby securely until the second arms are circled around the child.

Past friendships provide continuity to life as you reach out to establish new ones. Our highly mobile society may impose on us the premise that relationships are replaceable and temporary. Lifelong friendships are becoming increasingly rare. But the fractured and fragmented pattern of friendships that results from a series of moves can rob us of trusted friends, a sense of identity, and healthy intimacy. We must guard against loneliness, isolation, and detachment by being rooted in nurturing attachments.

There is a song youngsters often learn that offers sound advice: "Make new friends but keep the old. One is silver and the other is gold."

The Cycle of Readjustment

Everyone experiences some degree of confusion when they face the challenge of making a home in a new environment, especially those who make cross-cultural moves and must learn a new language and way of life. When we move to an unfamiliar community, we are confronted with new ways of doing things, new people, and new routines. We go into an intense learning mode and new information overload.

A friend of ours felt like a child. For a week she had to carry pieces of paper in her wallet so she could answer simple questions: "What is your address?" A new house number and zip code. "What is your telephone number?" She had three—one for their home, one for business, and a fax number. And because she lived near the border of two states, North and South Carolina, she had to memorize two new area codes and keep them differentiated. She felt like the kindergartner who wears a white tag!

Where can I buy groceries? Which doctor and dentist

do you recommend? Which school is the best choice? Which streets must I take to get there? Settling into the routine causes anxiety. These repeated occasions of disorientation, coupled with the loss of the familiar, bring about *culture shock.*

We generally think culture shock describes people who are living overseas, facing the challenges of adapting to a foreign culture. Yet there are cultural adjustments when you move from a small farming community to a large city, from a town of German heritage to a predominantly Italian neighborhood, or from the Midwest to the East Coast.

The intensity of the shock varies, of course, depending upon the amount of similarity to the former culture. But you may experience reactions characteristic of culture shock whenever you change communities. This period can be described as a cycle of readjustment generally marked by the following four phases.

Think about a move you made in your childhood or later in life. As you read through each description, try to identify specific memories that seem to fit the four phases. If you have recently relocated, decide where you are now in this cycle. What leads you to believe you are in this stage? How can you smooth the way through the next phases?

1. In the beginning people go through a euphoric period, sometimes nicknamed the "tourist" or "honeymoon" stage. We are excited about the move and show enthusiasm toward our new job, new home, and the adventure of meeting new friends.

2. In phase two the newness begins to wear off, and certain elements of the new situation begin to intrude into our lives. We experience frustration, anger, and depression. Bickering or withdrawal may

occur in the family, and job performance may be impeded.

3. The third phase of the readjustment cycle comes when the individual or family begins to take steps to change and to adapt. We learn to accept local ways and to establish new connections.

4. In phase four, we come to feel at home and to truly enjoy the new culture or community. We adjust our expectations to reflect reality, seeing both the benefits and the drawbacks of our new location.

Being aware of these normal stages of adjustment can make the move easier on your relationships. It is also helpful to get the daily newspaper even if you don't normally read one. In addition to local news, the paper will provide information about local shopping that you cannot glean from the telephone directory. By looking over the advertisements, you can become more familiar with the type of stores found near you and how to get there.

Moving can be an enjoyable, exciting experience. Flexible people who make friends easily often take the relocation in stride, feeling little if any anxiety. It helps to keep a sense of humor and be willing to learn about your new community. Communication skills, especially the ability to share your feelings, will also ease the transition.

Some individuals, however, will not be content no matter where they are. If you fantasize that the grass will always be greener somewhere else, you will have a hard time adjusting in any location. Other people are moving on the heels of a traumatic event to escape emotional pain. Studies show that many people feel that only by escaping can they recover from the death of a loved one or an unhappy episode in their life.

Excess Baggage

In many ways people take their problems with them when they move. This excess emotional baggage encumbers new relationships and drains the strength needed for the present. We cannot simply walk away from broken or damaged relationships. They follow us, and the real or perceived offenses from the past taint our present relationships and color our perceptions. Through personal counseling, many people discover that their emotional pain did not originate with the adjustments of moving. Kay realized that her move was only the trigger event that exposed unresolved tension.

"My problems stemmed from deep-rooted issues in my past (emotional neglect, issues from my childhood). My relocation to Minneapolis only caused these issues to *finally* surface. For years I had stuffed my anger, denied my feelings, and fell into the martyr syndrome. My coping strategy was summarized: Don't feel. Don't think. Don't trust. I remained frozen inside, thinking that if circumstances changed I could thaw out and get back to normal."

But merely changing circumstances will not heal a wounded heart. Hurt people repeat their history or relive it through compulsive retelling. In times of anxiety the mind seeks a resolution to past pain, locking people in the same old story with a misguided hope that somehow things will be different this time. The replay comes because the person has never really dealt with the trauma of the past.

Kay's struggle to have a productive relationship with her boss was complicated by her deep mistrust of male authority figures. She learned that her mistrust was the result of her father's controlling and abusive behavior. Other complex relational problems stemmed from her unmet emotional needs.

All unresolved experiences are not as dramatic or emotional as sexual abuse or drug and alcohol dependency issues. In fact, much of the time it is a case of hurt feelings or a betrayal of trust that snares people. "Once burned, twice shy," the saying goes. If we are disappointed, we find it difficult to commit on the same level of trust again. But building relationships without commitment and trust is as safe as building a brick tower without mortar.

Instead of dealing with the inability to commit or to trust, people may abandon a relationship or avoid bonding with others. We may feel hollow, unmotivated, or frozen inside; we shut down or put up protective walls—walls we can't reach over or let others through. We oppose ourselves in the desire to love and be loved, repeating the history of relational breakdown. A change of location will not destroy this destructive pattern; it takes a change of heart.

To avoid dragging emotional baggage along with you, it is necessary to change self-defeating behavior and to disconnect yourself from the source of the symptoms. Here are some effective steps to take. Keep your relationships in mind as you read.

Step 1 *Face up to any resentments or hurts you feel because someone has offended you or betrayed your trust, and admit any damage you have caused in relationships.*

Are you avoiding some people? Why? Are you angry with anyone?

Step 2 *Accept your responsibility in the matter.*

If you were at fault, apologize and restore the relationship if possible. If you were the victim of someone else's thoughtless words or actions, then accept your responsibility for how you have *responded* over the days, weeks, or years. Even if someone hurt you unjustly, you are still responsible for how you handle feelings of hatred, resentment, or anger.

Step 3 *Forgive everyone involved, yourself included. You must let go of the need to get even, and release your pain, resentment, and bitterness.*

Commit the person you hold accountable to God; let go of the need for revenge or punishment. Forgiveness does not mean that you set the other person free from the consequences of his behavior or absolve the guilty party of responsibility for his actions. Forgiveness is not pretending that what happened wasn't so terrible, or attempting to diminish and discount the damage. Forgiveness is honestly facing up to the truth, guilt, hurt, and shame then relinquishing it to God.

We pack our problems with us deliberately, more often than not, because we are unwilling to let go of past offenses, to risk being hurt again, or to learn new patterns of relating. We would rather stay offended and have a story to tell to invoke the sympathies of others. We prefer talking about the problem to solving it. Or we want to nurse a grudge and blame someone more than we want to be reconciled. By doing so we lose out on the joyous freedom of entering new relationships without destructive emotional baggage.

Moving can be a rewarding experience if we pack our luggage full of fond memories, meaningful traditions, insight gained, and lessons learned. Anger, offenses, and resentment are better left behind. Looking back on her difficult adjustments in Minneapolis and her return to California, Kay reflects, "I returned emotionally and physically exhausted. But only then was I ready to take the first real steps on the road to recovery. In that way the move was worth it. I'm a healthier, happier person now than I've ever been. I've learned to recognize the red flags that indicate when underlying emotional issues are prompting my behavior. And I've learned to set more realistic expectations. So I'll enjoy richer, more satisfying relationships no matter where I live in the future. I don't have to race off to somewhere in search of emotional health. I've learned that fresh starts don't begin with a change in location—they begin inside."

12

Critical Illness

Erin experienced a series of more typical childhood health problems after her heart surgery at age three: chicken pox, ear infections, and reoccurring strep throat, which led to a tonsillectomy. Her checkups were routine for a child her age except for extra blood work, angiograms, and echocardiograms. When she turned eight, surgery was scheduled to connect her heart to her lungs, artificially replacing the trunk of the pulmonary artery. Arlan and Rita were told there was a chance they could do the procedure in one operation rather than the repair stages they had previously expected.

Rita recalls the day of the surgery, "When the surgeon and his assistant, still dressed in scrubs, stepped up to the door of the cardiac intensive care waiting room, all eyes turned to them. Arlan and I immediately recognized him and moved quickly across the room for the first word of how Erin's open-heart surgery had gone. Dr. Puga motioned us into the hall and reported, 'The surgery went well, but we were unable to complete the repair. In three to six months you will need to bring her back, and we'll do the homograft [reconstruction using donor tissue] then.'

"It's been nearly a year since then, and we are still on hold. Although the reports keep changing, at Erin's most recent appointment our cardiologist told us we could expect to wait another year, possibly even two. We're thankful for Erin's good report and for the extended time to regroup before the next surgery. Even so, the news was unexpected and it feels a little like running in a cross-country race where someone keeps changing the route and moving the finish line—just when it appears within reach.

"But in the nine years since Erin's birth, we've learned that the finish line is an illusion," Rita adds. For families who have been touched by a major medical trauma, things never really go back to normal as it was defined before. That's not necessarily such a bad consequence. Suffering gives ample opportunity for character development and personal growth. Some families come out of their trials stronger and more appreciative than ever.

THE ACHE INSIDE

Individuals who have never encountered tragedy on a personal level usually have a general faith in good fortune, a carefree lack of anxiety based on the unspoken assumption *it will never happen to me.* The American Cancer Society reports that cancer will be diagnosed in 1 out of 3 Americans; 3 out of 4 families will have someone stricken by cancer.[1] These sobering facts alone show that *it will* happen to you—you or someone you love. No one is immune from pain or illness.

When a crisis does occur, we are no longer naive. We

know that we are not exempt from pain and sorrow. We ache inside over the loss.

Four years ago Elizabeth Berg was diagnosed as having an immune system cancer. In an article entitled "Moments of Ease," she wrote, "You look at photographs of yourself from before, aching. It is as though the essence of you has moved away, leaving behind a fragile shell that waits in vain to be what it used to be. You think you'll never be careless again, that you'll never laugh all the way, or lean back in your chair sighing and smiling, eyes closed, arms loose at your sides, *full of some naive sort of confidence you didn't know you had until you lost it*" (emphasis added).[2]

Even mature people with strong religious convictions can subtly confuse that breezy, "naive sort of confidence" with faith. When they can no longer accept that everything is going to work out right, when they lose their faith in good fortune, then it may appear that they have lost their faith *in God*. Some people confuse God with life—when they become disappointed with life, they become disappointed with God too. When life is not good, they jump to the thought that God is not good.

Although we may feel vulnerable and badly shaken when our sense of security is lost, the loss of our false confidence need not interrupt our relationship with God. God never gave a lifetime guarantee of good health. A mature faith has to rest on a deeper level of loving God for *who He is* and not just for *what He does or does not do* in this particular moment to ease our pain.

Critical illness strips away the veneer that we are in control of our lives. It uncovers our complete dependence upon the Creator of life. During that fragile time of sorting through emotions and working through our questions about God's involvement, many misunderstandings can arise that cause inner pain and a rift in our relationship with God. These misunderstandings may spring from our own misconceptions of God's character. Or the well-meant remarks of friends can touch a very sensitive spiritual nerve.

In a radio interview, Dr. James Dobson commented: "It's been my experience at the hospital that those who are going through suffering and pain, or what's sometimes worse, those whose children are going through life-threatening experiences like that, often already have a tremendous cross to bear. And then Christians —well-meaning Christians who really believe they are doing right—make it worse by saying those kinds of things that give them an emotional burden to carry in addition to what they already have."[3]

For example, a nonsupportive comment may place blame on the sick person or their family, implying, "You wouldn't be going through this if you hadn't displeased God. There must be sin in your life. You need to confess so that God can answer your prayers." But Job's story clearly demonstrates disaster can strike the innocent and give no indication of God's displeasure.

Another misunderstanding is expressed in remarks like this one a friend made to Rita: "Sickness is never God's will. God will heal Erin if you only believe and pray. You have to have faith." It is not necessarily a person's faith that is at fault. God can work miracles, but God also chose *not* to heal Paul: "My grace is sufficient for you, for My strength is made perfect in weakness" (2 Cor. 12:9).

Philip Yancey, author of *Where Is God When It Hurts?*, explained in a radio interview, "Jesus made very clear that He was not setting up a different category of human beings called 'Christians' who would have a different experience in life. In other words, He wasn't saying that from now on germ cells won't attack

Christians if you believe in Me. From now on tornadoes will hop over your houses. The tidal wave will mysteriously fold around your homes. We are a part of this world—part of this world that has been stained by the fall of man—and Jesus is saying 'Live out your faith in the midst of this world.' "[4]

When many questions were swirling around in her mind, Rita looked for reassuring verses like, "The LORD is good to those who wait for Him,/To the soul who seeks Him. . . . /Though He causes grief,/Yet He will show compassion/According to the multitude of His mercies./For He does not afflict willingly,/Nor grieve the children of men" (Lam. 3:25, 32–33).

RELATIONSHIPS FREED FROM SUPERFICIAL VALUES

Long after the diagnosis is in or the surgery is over, you will find that a close encounter with critical illness has altered your circumstances and how you relate to one another. Often those changes are a result of personal growth as well as the physical condition. People facing a loss of health may gain insight that leads to changed values and a greater emphasis on relationships.

At age eighteen, playwright Libba Bray was in a car accident that led to thirteen reconstructive surgeries. Her accident prompted her to shed a superficial value system: "I realized that all my life I had been thinking, *If only I can lose those 10 pounds/grow my hair out/ stop chewing my nails—then I'll be perfect.* Finally, my artificial eye allowed me to see that I would never reach that ideal. It was terrifying . . . and very liberating. I was free to step off the Treadmill of the Beautiful and into a wonderful world of mismatched eyes, crooked smiles, and size-8 hips. And I have never looked back."[5]

Like Libba, you will find your relationships enriched if you give up the idea that a person's value or identity is tied to their physical strength, stamina, or beauty. Focus instead on the inner person—character, spirit, and heart.

If you or someone you love is suffering from intense medical problems, you will also need to confront and think through common deceptions our culture promotes. Confront performance-based acceptance. (A man's work is not his worth; a woman's productivity does not define her identity.) Confront the quick fix and fast lane society that breeds frustration when we are forced to rest and wait, to be patient and endure. Confront the glorified stress on youth and power that implies that the old or handicapped, bedridden or nonathletic, are somehow second-class citizens. And face off against the imbalanced emphasis our culture places on independence and individualism.

In *You Gotta Keep Dancin'*, Tim Hansel writes about his own journey through intense daily pain: "Perhaps God gives us difficulties in order to give us the opportunity to know who we really are and who we really can be. We live in a world that is sometimes constipated by its own superficiality. But life's difficulties are even a privilege, in that they allow us or force us to break through the superficiality to the deeper life within."[6]

Changing Priorities

Beth Leuder, in her article "Through the Pain," talks candidly about her needs after back injuries that left her in chronic pain: "Difficulties have taught me to admit I need others. For most of my life I have been hesitant to let people into my struggles. Perhaps because of my own pride and fear of rejection. Or perhaps because it's unacceptable with some Christians to express true feelings about tribulations.

"The cloak of denial I was wrapped in tattered when I began to be honest with God and others. I found freedom in admitting I was weak and in need of prayer and encouragement. Time after time, as I've let friends into my world of pain, they have been God's hands to bring me comfort and hope. True, some people will never understand my ongoing bout with pain and discouragement. And I cannot expect them to. But it's still OK for me to practice gut-level honesty with close confidants . . . and with the Lord."[7]

A crisis situation often encourages us, as it did Beth, Arlan, and Rita, to admit our need for people and to put a higher priority on relationships. In healthy relationships increased appreciation and expressions of love help balance the shared pain and fear. The ordeal binds us together. One teenager, whose father suffered a massive heart attack, says, "We appreciate life and each other more, much more than I think other families do. We tell Dad that we love him every day, and he tells us. When I leave home in the morning and when I come back, I'm just glad to see Dad there. I think it's drawn us all closer."

Families that develop strength through crisis also learn to place a higher priority on communication. They talk about their fears. For Beth Leuder there are times when she is "afraid of more tests, more doctors, more pain, more time off work, more bed rest, more debt, more paperwork, more legal complications, more tears, more lonely times, more insurance hassles, more false hope."[8]

There is so much more involved than "Are you feeling better today?"

Talk things through. Suppressed emotions often result in depression, isolation, hopelessness, resentment —or more medical complications such as ulcers and headaches. In family counseling sessions at the clinic patients and family members learn how to better communicate feelings of anger, frustration, and fear—how not to keep everything bottled up inside. This is not to imply, however, that *every* negative feeling you experience should be indiscriminately dumped on those around you. The focus is on more understanding and appropriate sharing of feelings. And skills forged in the crucible of crisis serve the family well long into the future.

Fear, regret, and blame often mingle with the medical problems a family faces. A woman might blame herself for not finding her husband sooner after a stroke. A father regrets giving the car keys to his teenage son after an automobile accident. Or the families of cardiac patients may live with the constant fear that they will do or say something that will overexert or upset the patient, bringing on a fatal collapse. The listening ear and reassurance of a pastor, friend, or family member can help those working through overwhelming feelings.

Of course, close families that communicate well beforehand have a distinct advantage. As Pastor Charles Swindoll put it, "We cannot prepare for a crisis *after* that crisis occurs. Preparation must take place *before* we are nose to nose with the issue." Ideally, every family member should be taught good listening skills from an early age. It is essential for adults to learn how to discuss emotional issues. Adults as well as children should be encouraged to use the "I feel" format: "I feel (scared) when (Mom has to go back to the doctor)." Children can be encouraged to use artwork and storytelling to express their feelings.

Families who endure a crisis also place a higher priority on being together. After being diagnosed with cancer, Elizabeth Berg wrote poignantly, "You think you'll never yell at your children again. Everything they do seems so wonderful, so full of meaning, so close to being lost. You spend more time with them in the day, listen to them with all of yourself rather than half."[9]

Ironically, this increased tenderness and desire for togetherness can contribute to the stress of the situation. You may say you will never yell at your children again then the lack of sleep or mounting frustrations make you irritable. Trivial things irk you. Medications alter your moods. The guilt of responding in ways you never wanted to can add an extra burden. Especially now, you must be willing to forgive and to make allowance for each other. There are no perfect patients or caregivers. Be gentle toward one another. Don't be too hard on yourself.

Try to remain flexible when your desire for togetherness conflicts with other responsibilities. Dolores Curran, in her excellent book *Traits of a Healthy Family*, says that lack of time is possibly the most pervasive enemy the healthy family has. The illness of a family member compounds the problem. Insurance paperwork, hospital visits, and work all take time. Each family must arrive at workable compromises that allow for the emotional and physical needs of all family members, not just the needs of the individual facing medical problems.

Living with the Losses

And as the stricken person recovers, he must be eased into carrying his own load again. Don't let your desire to take care of someone degenerate into unhealthy overprotection or foster long-term dependence. There is a place, a noble place, for sacrificial love. But recovery requires allowing a person to regain as much as possible of what was lost—to again assume responsibility for her own schedule, behavior, feelings, and choices. Even though you are together on the tightrope of stress, you must refuse to carry someone who needs to regain emotional and physical strength by standing on her own two feet.

The day she came home from the hospital, Erin wanted not only to stand on her own two feet, but to ride her skateboard and her bike around the farm! Her mother would have preferred that she quietly read every story and poem in the *Childcraft* encyclopedia then go outside to play sometime next year, or at least wait a couple weeks. It took compromise from both sides to avoid overprotection and set reasonable limits on Erin's activities.

Total recovery, however, is not an essential requirement for healthy relationships. Steve, an engineer in his late forties, came into Dr. Fowler's office knowing his wife would never recover. He was concerned about his relationship with his twenty-five-year-old son, who would not come to visit Steve and his wife anymore. The family history revealed that Steve's wife was in a terrible car accident five years earlier. She recovered physically but never regained her preaccident status mentally. She now had a five-minute memory, would forget who her son was, and had to be placed in a day care center while Steve was at work.

Steve's wife could no longer respond to him emotionally, spiritually, or sexually. But he chose to accept what he could not change and to stay true to his vow "for better or worse, in sickness and in health." He expended his energy by running and competed in the Boston Marathon and other major runs. Steve's son, however, chose to deal with his mom by detachment, "out of sight, out of mind." He deserted his family.

When faced with overwhelming circumstances,

nearly everyone faces the temptation to take what initially appears to be the easier way out—to run away, emotionally withdraw, or detach. Some, like Steve, will choose to see their loved one through eyes of commitment and unconditional love. They will choose courage.

Relationships deepen as people determine that they will live with unavoidable losses and separations. In *A Path Through Suffering*, Elisabeth Elliot writes insightfully about the separation between health and sickness: "There is a fellowship among those who suffer, for they live in a world separated from the rest of us. When my husband Addison Leitch was dying of cancer he felt keenly the impossibility of my understanding his experience. 'It's two different worlds we're living in,' he said, 'and there's no commerce between the two.' He could not help feeling that I did not care enough. I cared as much as a wife can care for a husband she adores and cannot bear to lose, but it was not enough. I did not know what Add knew. I had not been there. When we went to the waiting room of the radiation department at the hospital, however, we met others who *knew*—a little boy with red X's on his temples, a man whose lower jaw had been removed."[10]

As the parent at the bedside of a sick child, you may long, as Rita and Arlan did, to somehow trade places. You ache for the chance to take the pain upon yourself and spare your child. But of course you cannot. Your loved one is caught in a body separate from yours, and you cannot enter their experience to the degree compassion compels. Support from others who have encountered similar circumstances can be of great help at such times, although you may not have the strength to endure the sadness of anyone else's story at first.

With life-threatening or disabling illness you may also lose cherished parts of life—the traditional father figure role, the opportunity to be homemaker, or the carefree childhood most little girls and boys take for granted. Besides this, the patient may lose control over certain aspects of his physical body. After his stroke, award-winning novelist Paul West wrote, "It is as if I am my own laboratory specimen, over which I have no control. Indeed, being a novelist, I now regard my medical self as one of my characters, whose every tremor and twinge I monitor."[11] For relationships to remain strong, family members must adapt to these changes and remain flexible.

There is no superglue for putting your life back together after illness or trauma has intruded, shattering your dreams and security. Recovering and learning to live with permanent losses take time.

Here are ways you can help hurting families endure the day-to-day pains that inevitably come from living in an imperfect world. If you know of someone who currently needs your help, keep them in mind as you read. Check what you can do to help.

____ *Allow family members freedom to work through their own emotions.* Both the initial diagnosis and the crisis of hospitalization can prompt a variety of feelings. Ranging from anger, worry, and frustration to tenderness, compassion, and helplessness, these emotions mingle into a blur of stress. Let them handle that stress in the way that works best for them—not what seems best to you.

____ *Encourage exercise.* Plan a brisk walk or a chance to climb stairs. Resist the urge to tell a friend, "What you need is a good cry." Maybe what she *really* needs is a good aerobic workout!

____ *Allow plenty of time for emotions to stabilize.* Unlike the episodes of daytime TV dramas, real-life emotions seldom resolve within thirty minutes. Expecting a speedy resolution can make family members feel pressured to pretend.

____ *Encourage the patient and family to ask their physi-cian the emotionally charged questions that may be gnawing at their peace of mind.* "Can the defect be traced to something in pregnancy?" "What happens next?" "Why do the nurses seem so concerned?" If the family is uneasy with the diagnosis or treatment, the vital question they may be reluctant to ask their doctor is "Who would you recommend for a second opinion?"

____ *Create a supportive home environment.* Understand-ably, more attention is focused on the physical and emo-tional needs of the patient and those who stay at the hospital with him. But the family members left trying to maintain a normal work routine while inwardly ach-ing also need support. Remain alert to opportunities to help out at home.

____ *Really listen to the patient and family members.* Many people avoid visits because they do not know what to say, but often the most helpful thing you can do is listen. Just being there to offer an understanding ear can lessen the lonely ordeal the family faces.

____ *Help the family keep up with responsibilities on a day-to-day basis.* Life goes on. Families facing medical prob-lems may also be burdened by finances, keeping up on the job, and the details of staying in the hospital or rehabilitation center, especially if travel is required. It is here that listening friends can be of great help. As you sense a need, you can ask specific questions and offer help: Suggest that you drive them to and from chemotherapy, pick up Grandma at the airport, or get their little girl to a classmate's birthday party. Do what-ever the recipients perceive as helpful—not what you think they ought to appreciate. These loving gestures will demonstrate genuine understanding and support. Doing little things can be a big encouragement!

____ *If you are unsure what to do or say, send a personal note.* A letter or card is a universally accepted expres-sion of care that can strengthen your relationship and provide encouragement. One that deeply touched Rita was from a little boy named Zachary, a friend of Erin's.

When Erin was transferred from intensive care following open-heart surgery in Rochester, three hundred miles from home, Zachary sent her a picture. In the corner he had carefully printed "To Erin" in bright crayon letters. Underneath he had drawn a little blonde-haired girl in a hospital bed—with guardian angels circling above her.

13

Divorce or Widowhood

Randall was five feet, ten inches, although his trim physique and square shoulders gave the impression that he was taller. He spoke quietly, occasionally looking toward the window or the floor, as he summarized the problems he faced following his divorce: "Externally I faced the adjustment of going from married life to being a single parent, the uncertainty of not knowing who would get the kids, and the frustration of not having them as much as I was used to. Internally I faced rejection from the one I committed my life to and the disbelief that it was actually happening to me."

Randall touches on several significant issues that commonly surface following divorce, especially for people like him who did not want to break up the marriage but were left to pick up the pieces.

ACCEPTING THE ROLES AND RESPONSIBILITIES OF A SINGLE ADULT

One of the hardest adjustments for Randall was accepting the finality of the divorce. He wanted the marriage to be restored so badly that his heart was clinging to the hope of reconciliation, even though as time passed his former spouse gave no indication they would ever get back together. Although the willingness to forgive and reconcile is noble and even biblical, a desperate, obsessive desire to mend the marriage can lead to magical thinking, bargaining with God, or putting life on hold.

After going through the stages of grief, there comes a time when the divorced person must look back, consider what went wrong and what role he had in the problems, learn from the painful lesson, and move on. The individual must recognize and separate her identity from that of the former spouse and turn from the broken marriage to wholesome singleness. This does not mean that the person gives up on God's ability to change the spouse but rather leaves the past and present relationship in God's hands and goes on about life. It is a painful process.

Unfortunately, when family ties unravel, this process of separation is often marred by power struggles, judgmental attitudes, and manipulative attempts at controlling—often at the expense of the children. If you are still trying to have your needs (for love, respect, conversation, intimacy, companionship, security) met through the relationship, remind yourself that your former mate *does not have to change* for your sake. He is not committed to you and tied to your well-being as he once was. She now has interests and choices you have no part in. You must begin to make choices and build a life independent of her behavior.

Whether you lost your spouse through death or divorce, you can choose to cherish the good memories and move on with life. Be aware that many people tend to view their new role in a conditional way that depends on the behavior of their former spouse. A widow might think to herself, *Charlie wouldn't like it if I sold the business*. Examine your actions to make sure they are not overly dependent on, or vulnerable to, the real or imagined response of an absent spouse.

Individuals who lose their mate through divorce or death sometimes refuse to shed old roles and accept personal responsibility for their new life on their own.

Mildred is an example of someone who refused to shed old roles. She had always been the giving partner in her marriage. Mildred's husband was a strong, harsh, outspoken man who dominated her, making all decisions large and small. Yet Mildred had always seemed cheerful and comfortable in the relationship. Her husband had a heart attack and died suddenly when they were in their early sixties. Mildred held up well enough during the first few weeks following his death while others clustered around her offering support, but after that she became a recluse. When she broke her hip four years later and had to be hospitalized, her niece made some unsettling discoveries.

Mildred's home had become filthy. Mail, newspapers, microwave dinner plates, and other small food containers were piled everywhere. Mildred, it seems, could not even make such small decisions as what type of cleaning product to use or what to keep and what to discard. After her hip mended, doctors recommended that her niece admit her to a nursing home facility because she seemed incapable of handling the normal routines of life. She was as sweetly docile as ever and could speak coherently and understand. Yet she was unable to carry on the affairs of daily adult life. She didn't want to grow out of dysfunctional dependency.

Carol was also in her early sixties when she lost her husband of forty years to cancer. She had always struggled with her weight and blood pressure and found little enjoyment in exercise. She, too, held up well during the initial weeks following her husband's death, but she began to battle depression about six months later.

Her daughter convinced Carol to come spend some time with her in California. There, away from her normal routine and home life, Carol began to make some changes in her eating habits. Her daughter enjoyed walking, so they walked together quite often. After about a month Carol noticed that she had more energy and her clothes were looser. By the end of six months Carol had made new friends, improved her health and disposition, and shed about twenty-five pounds. Her blood pressure was well within normal range, and she was adjusting to the daily pressures of life as a single woman.

Living out a new role may seem threatening, but there is no going back. You have to face the loss and move on to make choices. With God's help you can move from pain to peace—and establish rewarding, loving relationships with others.

Responses that Hinder Relationships

When you are used to sharing your life with someone, lack of companionship can leave you feeling empty, lonesome, and sad. After living in a world geared for couples, even previous friendship patterns are altered. Often the initial response is counter-productive.

Barbara was in her thirties when her husband, a prominent businessman, was killed in a plane crash. They had been involved in a couple's bridge club and couple's tennis league, and they socialized at corporate and chamber of commerce parties. In the accident Barbara not only lost her husband, but also she lost her social life and friendship network. No longer invited to corporate get-togethers, Barbara lost touch with her husband's former colleagues and their families. She dropped out of the tennis league and bridge club. Her reaction was passive: she felt sorry for herself.

Based on his years of counseling experience, Dr. Fowler can draw the following insights and suggest these action points for Barbara. His goal is to direct her toward a response alternative that leads to healthy relationships. Can you identify with the wisdom of his words? Is there an application to your own situation regardless of the crisis you face?

Taking the Initiative to Stay Connected

"If Barbara were to enter my office," Dr. Fowler suggests, "I would try to help her see the possibilities and opportunities still out there for her." Although her inclination might be to bow out of life to nurse her wounds, Dr. Fowler stresses that she needs to take the initiative to stay connected with others. Perhaps she did feel like the odd man out in the context of the couple's clubs. We do have to accept that some parts of life must ultimately change, but they need not be eliminated. If she still enjoys tennis, she should definitely seek other opportunities to play in single's leagues or with another friend.

Barbara must also accept the fact that she may need to reach out and become involved in other groups to feel fulfilled and nurtured at this time. Certainly a Bible-believing church with a strong ministry to widowed and single people would be a good place to start.

Finally, it seems Barbara may be "projecting"—that is, assuming that people feel a certain way when there is no real basis in fact for those feelings. Barbara should not simply assume that the people she and her husband had been friends with no longer want to spend time with her. They may want very much to continue to be a part of Barbara's life. She must be careful not to close off those old friends who could give her some much-needed support and validate the former identity that remains a very real part of her. It could be comforting for Barbara to talk with those who remember her husband and recall the good times they spent together.

Getting Rid of Bitterness, Anger, and Slander

Gene lived in the small town where his wife grew up. After their divorce many friends and acquaintances chose sides with his wife and resisted his efforts to maintain contact. His response was aggressive: he was angry and put the blame on the community. He had nothing good to say about his former wife or her hometown. He left, determined to make a sophisticated place for himself in the world, then come back to snub them and get even.

Gene's main problem is bitterness. If he allows himself to be controlled and motivated by this emotion, he is in for far greater struggle and sadness. It is important for Gene to face his anger and bitterness and consciously reject the emotion, actions, and words inspired by it.

Gene must also resist the urge to injure the reputation of his former wife and community. Putting them down will not build him up. He must let go of the idea that he has something to prove to them. As long as his words and behaviors are *reactive*, Gene's present life will be controlled by his past.

Instead, Gene needs to bring his energies to bear on

building a new life for himself. He needs to set aside time every day to study and memorize Scripture, especially asking God to help him to forgive those who have wronged him. By releasing past relationships to God, he is then free to focus on ways to construct new relationships through his employment, church, and social organizations. A positive, thankful spirit goes a long way toward making you the kind of person others naturally want to get to know.

Renewing Your Mind

Jill was involved in an abusive marriage that progressively grew worse. Looking back, she explains, "As the abuse continued, I became more centralized on the two of us—concentrating on working it out, seeking God's will and intervention for our lives. I shared our problems, our crisis, our needs with no one. No one except God. Extended relationships were the bare minimum. I was not allowed to 'spend time with the girls' or socialize with anyone. Family relationships were across the ocean." Jill coped because she had to; it was a matter of survival. After the divorce she had to fight off self-destructive tendencies. "I was very hard on myself. I would cut myself down and chew myself out for the way I acted, lowering my self-esteem even more."

It is very important for Jill to change the negative inner messages leading her to believe certain things about herself and her world that are not true. The "I'm not doing things well enough," "I don't deserve any better," and "It's all my fault" messages must be replaced by positive, biblically correct beliefs that become just as ingrained. A new inner dialogue will allow Jill to see herself and her world in a new light: "God loves me and accepts me as I am." "I am a valuable person because God made me valuable." "I can control my choices but I can't control other people's choices."

Dr. Fowler would also encourage Jill to combat these feelings of inferiority by placing an imaginary E on the forehead of everyone she meets. The E stands for *equal in Christ*—in Christ no one is superior or inferior to her. Each person is on equal footing before God.

Jill needs to understand what caused those negative messages in her life. Then she needs to accept that her response to those initiating experiences was faulty— that her feelings were not in line with her worth in God's eyes. She should recognize, every day, that God wants her to know how precious she is to Him. Many verses deal with the believer's position of honor in Christ Jesus, and many more speak of His love and our value in His sight. Jill could meditate on and commit to memory these verses:

- *Self acceptance:* "I will praise You, for I am fearfully and wonderfully made; . . . my soul knows very well" (Ps. 139:14).
- *Acceptance:* "All that the Father gives Me will come to Me, and the one who comes to Me I will by no means cast out" (John 6:37).
- *Value to God:* "[C]asting all your care upon Him, for He cares for you" (1 Peter 5:7).

It would be helpful for Jill to begin keeping a journal of her daily experiences. In her journal she can determine when she has allowed "old tapes" to surface in her mind's recording and her reaction to them. A good mental exercise might be to replay an event when she has fallen into old ways of reacting, and decide how she could have responded instead. This will help her in future situations.

Reflect a moment on the different response patterns of Barbara, Gene, and Jill. Then speculate: How would you imagine each of them responding to rejection? Financial adjustments? Anxiety? Form an idea in your mind of how shame, guilt, failure, or low self-esteem might figure into their future behavior. It doesn't take long to reach the conclusion that feeling sorry for yourself, being motivated by anger, turning the hurt inward —and the other responses you imagined—will not lead to healthy, balanced relationships.

Grieving the Loss

Facing the devastating loss of someone you love is more traumatic than many people acknowledge even to themselves. The grieving process must cover a host of life changes. Give yourself a chance to identify and grieve for some of those losses by checking the statements below that apply to you.

____ *"I grieve the loss of my marriage and the companionship of my mate."*

____ *"I grieve the loss of my good health. Fatigue, headaches, or stomach pains seem to be a constant part of life."*

____ *"I grieve the loss of a good night's sleep—it seems impossible to put things out of my mind and to relax."*

____ *"I grieve the loss of money in the bank and financial security."*

____ *"I grieve the loss of feeling happy. I lack the spontaneity to find fun in life."*

____ *"I grieve the loss of my emotional health. Most of the time I feel emotionally drained or depressed before the day even begins."*

____ *"I grieve the lost time with my family. I feel as if I don't know my children anymore."*

____ *"I grieve the loss of a sexual relationship and marital intimacy."*

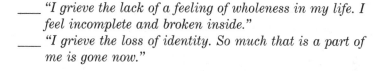

____ *"I grieve the lack of a feeling of wholeness in my life. I feel incomplete and broken inside."*

____ *"I grieve the loss of identity. So much that is a part of me is gone now."*

Although this exercise may seem depressing, it helps to openly acknowledge the losses you face. But don't stop there. Now make your own list beginning with the phrase: *"I'm thankful for the chance . . ."* Realize that you have opportunities and blessings as well as losses and sorrow. Here are a few statements to get you started:

____ *"I'm thankful for the chance to enjoy so many good times. No one can take away my good memories."*

____ *"I'm thankful for the chance to love my friends and family."*

____ *"I'm thankful for the chance to be alive and to live a satisfying life."*

When you are hurting, you have to make some decisions on how you will handle the pain. Will you allow it to destroy your friendships and distance you from other family members? Or will you work through your feelings in ways that bond you to others?

You do have choices. You can choose to face the losses. You can choose your attitude and the way you treat others. And you can ask God to bring good out of your grief. "The most important thing I would tell anyone in this situation is to get yourself right with the Lord," Randall explains. "That doesn't mean just praying or reading the Bible but having a personal relationship with Him that assures you that you are a complete and whole person in Christ. There's so much pain involved that you have to relieve it some way. I can remember sitting at home crying my guts out because it hurt so bad. But you have to give it over to the Lord and get your strength from Him. After a while things get better. I see a broken heart a lot like a broken arm. You have to treat it properly, but also time heals the hurt."

Part of treating your grief properly is to refuse to display your pain for all the world to see. Instead, share it with your closest friends who can truly respond with loving support. You can choose not to behave miserably even though you may feel miserable! People do not like complainers, and you need other people more than you need to publicly air your gripes.

Try to put yourself around others in constructive settings, as Randall did. "A small support group I attended was a positive step in my recovery. I needed to be around people who cared, and I received a lot of prayer support. In addition, I looked forward to times when friends would invite me over, even if it was for something small.

"At first I was consumed with the divorce and the problems that went with it. And I took my emotions out on others. But time and communication smoothed that out. God, my family, and my friends helped pull me through."

14

Financial Setbacks

Mike Carlson shook my hand firmly as he entered my office, then set his notebook on the corner of the desk. He said, Dr. Fowler recalls, "There it is," with an eagerness in his voice that suggested he was pleased with the work he and Patti had done. And Patti had a sparkle in her eye when she added excitedly, "Last week when you said that setting goals was an *excellent* communication tool you were up to mischief!"

"Hum? Not me! What makes you say that?" Dr. Fowler teased back, and then asked, "How did it go?" He already had a pretty good idea. It is often clear within the first few minutes of a counseling session how the previous week's assignment has gone, and from all indications their project had been a profitable one.

"Writing out our plan of action forced us to talk things through in specific terms. There were a few tense moments, but working through the conflicts made it clear that money wasn't the real issue," Mike answered. He picked up the notebook and pointed at the goals they had listed. "We wrote it out as you suggested: Long-term perspective/Short-term objective."

LONG-TERM PERSPECTIVE/
SHORT-TERM OBJECTIVE

The exercise Mike and Patti completed at the Minirth-Meier Clinic would be helpful to any family who is facing financial problems, whether those problems resulted from unexpected medical bills, loss of a job, or extenuating circumstances. The exercise was not complicated. Mike and Patti looked at the relative importance of the various problems we had identified in our discussions, chose the ones they felt were the most significant, and wrote down what they wanted to see happen in the long run—their flight plan. After listing the long-term perspective in these areas, they broke the goals down into short-term action steps.

From a long-term perspective, the Carlsons listed three goals. First, Mike wanted to secure employment that would provide a comfortable income for his family and utilize his past experience. His first short-term objective under that goal had already been accomplished. At Dr. Fowler's suggestion, Mike had invited five of his friends from different fields to a "brainstorming party" earlier that week. Together they had helped him think of types of jobs he should apply for, and offered input on his résumé rough draft. His second objective was to stay in touch with his friends for encouragement and accountability as well as possible employment leads. Mike's next action step was to get the résumé professionally produced and send out five to ten résumé packets each week. He wanted to become proactive—taking the initiative to solve their problems—rather than behaving reactively with a depressed outlook and victim mentality.

The second long-term goal Mike and Patti listed had to do with Mike's feelings of insecurity based on his childhood experiences. Their goal was to keep Mike's relationships with his father and mother on an adult-to-adult level, and to make the decisions they felt were best regardless of his parents' response. "We both agreed on our long-range goal for the health of our family," Mike said. "But then Patti suggested the first action step should be to refuse to accept any gifts or financial help from my parents regardless of how bad things became. I got defensive and said that her family didn't have enough money to help us out, so there wasn't much choice."

"What did you feel, Patti, when Mike drew your parents into the discussion?" Dr. Fowler asked.

"At first I felt angry at being shut off. Then I realized that we were falling into what you called the *binary trap*, where you focus on the question 'Should we do this or not?' as if saying yes or no are the only alternatives. And I realized the real question was 'Where is the best place for us to borrow money if it comes to that?' When I told Mike what I was thinking and put the question that way, we came up with more options to consider—none of which involved either set of parents."

"I'm proud of you Patti. That was a terrific way to handle things!" Dr. Fowler responded.

"When Patti rephrased the question it made me realize that I had subconsciously been thinking that I was trapped—that I had no choice but to fail without my parents' help," Mike added. "When I could see other options, I agreed that it would be best to leave my mom and dad out of it. Patti's second action point, that I always talk things through with her before asking my folks for advice, made sense in light of our long-term goal too. But it's not going to be easy for me to do."

For their third long-range goal, Mike and Patti listed getting out of debt and reestablishing a savings cushion that would tide them over if unexpected circumstances ever came up again. Their short-term plan was simply to reduce spending in several small ways they had worked out together and to pay off everything they had purchased on a payment plan or with credit cards, starting with the smallest bill first.

Balancing Your Accounts

The Carlsons were beginning to exhibit many characteristics of strong families—good communication, spiritual unity, appreciation, and commitment to each other. In *The Secrets of Strong Families*, Nick Stinnett and John DeFrain explain that these strengths "serve as a pool of resources that [strong families] draw on when times are difficult—rather like we save money for a 'rainy day.' In contrast, unhealthy families are worn out and depleted on a daily basis by the stress of poor relationships. When a crisis comes along, the unhealthy family must add it to the burden they already struggle with. No wonder the load is sometimes too much."[1]

The analogy between balance in a relationship and balance in a bank account is a helpful one. Words of appreciation, respect, time spent together, and thoughtful actions are all "deposits" into your relational account. They add to the strength and security of the bond. But taking one another for granted, criticizing, or unthoughtfulness deplete the account. For example, Mike's moodiness and emotional detachment from Patti drained their relationship, just as bills and house payments depleted their savings.

In financial terms, we all understand the need for a cash flow margin—having more money coming in than going out. In the same way, keeping a positive margin in a relational ledger *on a daily basis* is a key to building and maintaining balance. Refuse to run in the red for an extended time. If you drain the account with an outburst of anger, then counter the damage by saying you are sorry and asking for forgiveness. Praise each other often. Figure in times of refreshment and restoration.

When the Krajewski family went through a period of financial difficulties, tension began to mount between Mary Ann and her husband. But they took constructive steps to maintain their marriage. In response to our survey, Mary Ann wrote, "Larry and I made a commitment to never blame each other. It was very needed! I could not blame him and he could not blame me—we established a mutual trust fund."

In relationships, all interactions have a cumulative effect. The little things or seemingly insignificant irritations can empty an account. And when either person's needs remain unmet for an extended time, the relationship is at risk. The good news is that it works both ways. Even when you don't have much money, you can still nurture your relationships and fill your love accounts. In the good times you can continue to add to good memories so that you have something to fall back on the next time a situation puts a strain on your friendship or family.

Mike and Patti began to stabilize their love account when they started pulling together, talking things through, and adding the positive feelings of joint accomplishment. Here are some other practical ways to balance the draining effects of adversity and to keep money matters from driving a wedge in your relationship. Put a check by those you have already implemented.

_____ *Write out your financial goals.* As mentioned previously, writing out your goals encourages communication, clarifies your thoughts and feelings, and encourages joint effort.

___ *Pull together.* Have you ever tried to drive a car with the emergency brake on? That's a good description of the way many families initially work against themselves in the area of finances. One cuts back while another spends. One asks for professional advice while the other refuses to follow it. One makes decisions while another resists them. After a couple learns to keep the crisis in perspective and to work together at problem solving, the brake is released and forward movement is unhampered.

___ *Respond rationally, not emotionally.* People who seek counseling for overwhelming financial problems are often paralyzed by panic. They take no action because they are immobilized by the fear of making a mistake or by the conclusion that all effort is pointless. Or, they slide into an obsessive/compulsive cycle, where they are obsessed with their money problems at all times and handle it through compulsive behavior, for example, workaholism, stealing, deceitfulness. Rather than setting a deliberate course and following it, they tend to do only what they feel good about or what the circumstances force upon them. They respond to the emotion of the moment and make poor choices. In contrast, when individuals respond rationally to the financial facts, their relationships are more stable and their financial position generally improves.

___ *Seek wise counsel.* When your heart is breaking or you are under extreme stress, it is very difficult not to respond emotionally. Therefore it makes good sense to get an objective outside opinion and to avoid hasty decisions. Many churches offer inexpensive or free financial counseling. Hospitals and insurance companies will generally help answer questions and work through possible payment arrangements. Or the advice of a trusted friend, whose judgment you value, may help you make wise choices.

___ *Invite God's help.* John MacArthur extensively researched what the Bible had to say about money and then summarized, "16 out of 38 of Christ's parables deal with money; more is said in the New Testament about money than heaven and hell combined; five times more is said about money than prayer; and while there are 500 plus verses on both prayer and faith, there are over 2,000 verses dealing with money and possessions."[2] God repeatedly used practical illustrations with money to illustrate spiritual truth, making it clear His wisdom applies in both the spiritual and practical realms.

Many of us recognize that God has the wisdom and desire to help with our financial problems. But we are like a little boy who ran to his father saying, "This tag on the back of my shirt is bothering me." Then before the father could reach for the scissors, the little boy jerked the tag, tearing it loose from the shirt collar—and ripping a hole in the seam in the process. We say we are asking for help, but instead we are taking matters into our own hands because we are unwilling to wait. Beware of quick, impulsive decisions. They rarely solve financial problems.

____ *Allow others to express their love.* One of the ways we express our love and compassion for others when they are faced with adversity is to share our time, possessions, and money. Your community, church community, or friends may step in to shoulder some of your burden. If they do, appreciate their concern and accept their help.

But if no one offers assistance, ask yourself two questions before responding with frustration or bitterness: First, *Have I let my close companions know what my real situation is?* They may not be aware of the seriousness of your situation unless you have shared your concern. Don't assume they can read your mind or your bills.

And second, try to objectively consider: *Am I taking things too personally and unrealistically expecting too much?* Certain problems will always generate more compassionate response than others. For example, people often rally around a family whose house burned down or whose preschooler has cancer and needs expensive treatment. The needs incurred when a loved one is placed in a nursing home, however, will largely go overlooked. Be realistic about how much you expect from others.

____ *Recognize issues under the surface.* In our culture, money is tied very closely to issues of power and self-worth. What appears at first glance to be a problem with handling the stress of insufficient funds may really be a struggle with feelings of worthlessness, low self-esteem, or loss of identity through loss of financial status or employment. Tension also arises over financial concerns when one spouse feels an extreme need to control and uses money for leverage. Try to discern whether any of these factors are undermining your relationships.

It is often helpful to ask yourself: *In what ways have money matters complicated or eased my current circumstances? Do my attitudes toward money strengthen or divide my family? Are money problems only a symptom of personal problems that have not been resolved?*

____ *Keep a sense of humor.* Regardless of your bank account balance, a healthy dose of humor and a cheerful outlook will improve your relationships. Humor is a great antidote for stress as long as it is not cutting or sarcastic. Laughing together at inside jokes can bring much-needed breaks in the tension and reaffirm that "we're in this together." It is important to treat serious things seriously, but life's load will seem lighter if you can learn to see the humorous side of things too.

When Is Support Beneficial?

Although it is healthy to give and to receive help in times of trouble, not all help is good. There must be guidelines and limits. Here are some marks of beneficial support.

It Is Voluntary

Because of our love for others, we should freely desire to help them out. But if we are shamed into it by manipulation, pressure, or guilt, then it will not have the same positive effect on the relationship. On the receiving end, we must always be allowed the dignity of declining money. As Mike and Patti discerned, it was not in their best interest to accept money from Mike's parents. Don't give or receive money that has strings attached or will have a negative impact on the relationship in the future.

Don't Ask for Help Merely to Be Rescued

Sometimes it is easy to let someone else carry the baton when you are perfectly capable of running yourself. Also, resist the urge to rescue others without considering whether it is truly in their best interest. Don't give money in response to repeated cycles of urgent need because of poor financial planning. Laziness or irresponsible money management do not constitute legitimate reasons for receiving continued financial support. In such cases offer financial training and the encouragement to be responsible.

Marked by Gratitude and Humility

Healthy giving is characterized by an attitude of gratitude, humility, and love. We are to be thankful for the many blessings God has given that enable us to share with others. We are also to receive with gratitude and humility, thankful for God's willingness to meet our needs and the kindness of caring friends. There is no place for arrogant pride in demanding help or in smugly giving it.

Handled Quietly and with Dignity

When support is given in healthy ways, the dignity and respect of both parties involved is taken into consideration. Offering financial support should not call undue attention to either the one giving or the one receiving—neither should feel awkward or embarrassed. And the terms of the agreement, including the time frame for repayment if the money is loaned, should be clearly understood to prevent misunderstandings later.

Money given out of love and concern encourages, supports, and offers relief for people in need. In a truly loving relationship money will never be offered if it enables people to live irresponsibly, to shirk their duty toward their families, to foster a dysfunctional dependency, or to continue in any sinful life-style. Love will achieve the balance between two emotionally costly mistakes—taking too much responsibility for the feelings, behavior, and choices of others, or not taking enough responsibility for *our own*.

Concentrating on making the best of a bad financial situation is often the best coping strategy of all. Money was tight when Mike's birthday rolled around, but Patti refused to focus on the lack of presents or spoil the day moping. Instead she and the kids planned a surprise sand volleyball party at an area beach. When she invited close family friends, Patti requested that they bring snacks and soft drinks in place of gifts. Then Patti and the kids browsed through the line of contemporary cards at a local discount store and chose a birthday card for Mike. On the card was a goofy-looking man saying, "It's your birthday! Time to forget about your past—to forget about your future . . .

". . . but most importantly—forget about your present! ('cause this is it!) Happy Birthday."

Part III
It Can Be Done!

15

**Turning a Setback
into a Comeback**

A friend of ours has a beautiful antique rocking chair. It looks like a wonderful piece of fine furniture, and it rocks smoothly and quietly—but you can't sit down in it! The joints are not strong enough to bear the weight. In the same way, most adults look pretty good going through the motions characteristic of maturity. For the most part, we appear to operate our relationships in fine fashion—until the pressure comes. Then, as with the antique chair, areas of immaturity show up under stress, and bonds give way under the weight of adversity.

In times of trouble we find ourselves to be a mixture of nobility and selfishness, of courage and cowardice, of faith and hopelessness. In short, we find out there is still plenty of room for personal growth!

But we may feel too hopeless, helpless, angry, or tired to face the challenge. Often our relationships suffer not so much from our problems, or from a lack of information on how to handle them, as from a lack of motivation to change. When your problems seem insurmountable, remember what Sir Edmund Hillary, the first man to climb Mount Everest, said. "You don't have to be a fantastic hero to do certain things. . . . You can be just an ordinary chap, sufficiently motivated to reach challenging goals. The intense effort, the giving of everything you've got is a very pleasant bonus."

DON'T LOSE HEART

So don't lose heart—you don't know how the story will end. Ordinary people can overcome hardship. God can give a suddenly altered life new and solid meaning. Ten years from now you may look back on your current hardships and see them differently. Memories of the closeness with people you love and the lessons you've learned may ease the pain of your problems. Things could work out better than you think they will, as Gina can testify.

At age sixteen, the things Gina enjoyed doing most were playing the piano and writing and singing songs. So when it came time to make plans for after high school, the logical choice was music. She decided to go to the university to study piano and voice performance. But before she could pursue this goal, she had a problem she needed to deal with. Gina had nodules on her vocal cords that were causing her to speak with a very raspy voice and to occasionally lose her voice altogether.

The surgery to remove the nodules was expected to result in a much clearer speaking and singing voice. Gina's doctor told her she would be singing in two weeks. No big deal. She had the surgery the summer before her senior year of high school. Gina recalls, "The results were far from what I was told to expect. I was unable to speak. For the first week after the surgery, I could make virtually no sounds whatsoever. When I did try to talk, it sounded like a strained whisper. I was terrified of what was happening to me. Not only was the fear and frustration hard to deal with, but I was practically abandoned by my doctor. We were unable to reach him for days, and when we did, he gave us no explanation, no advice. No help at all.

"I was more discouraged than I had ever been in my life," Gina continues. "I knew early on that this experience was going to affect me in ways I had never expected. My plans were being changed drastically, and I wasn't too happy about it! I hoped that God knew what He was doing, because I was lost."

Over the next six months Gina saw three different specialists who prescribed voice rest when she couldn't even attempt to talk. Her vocal cords were very swollen and irritated after the operation, and because her first doctor told her to start talking immediately following surgery, she had scar tissue that was actually worse than the nodules ever were. Gina ended up going through six months of intense speech therapy in order to learn how to talk again.

Tapes of the early speech therapy sessions record Gina's heartbreaking efforts. When asked by the therapist to sing the simple children's song, "Mary Had a Little Lamb," Gina struggled to produce a halting series of sounds on wandering pitches, "Ma . . . ri . . . haa . . ."

"Most of my family and friends were very supportive

throughout the whole ordeal," Gina says. "My closest friends would call me on the phone and just talk to me. Sometimes my mom would act as my interpreter, and other times I would respond by whistling once for yes and twice for no. Of course there were times when people were very cruel, making jokes and not realizing how much hurt I was feeling. Those were the times when I would just go home and cry with my mom, as we sat and wondered where all of this was leading. God allowed me to experience love in some very special ways through my family and close friends. I must have been terribly boring to be around, but they put up with me and helped encourage me through the most discouraging days.

"During those weeks and months of not knowing what the future would hold for me, God was dealing with much more than just my physical condition," Gina adds. "At the time, however, it was often hard to look past the actual physical limitations of not being able to talk. In tough times, it's easy to focus our vision on the problem at hand and not look at the bigger picture and how God can use our problems for His glory." Ten months passed before Gina was singing again at all, and about two-and-a-half years of hard work were required before she was back to her normal voice and range.

Four-and-a-half years after the surgery Gina was recording her first album! She reports, "While I was working on that album, I went in for a checkup. Miraculously, the scar tissue had disappeared. God had led me through those difficult times and was now leading me on to show His purpose for it all. He had given me my voice back, and it actually was better than before. I had learned what it meant to really trust God with my life—to trust that He can see the bigger picture and can use a bad situation and turn it around for good. I also learned to rely on the people God had placed in my life. He has blessed me with friends and family who are genuinely concerned about my well-being. And God has blessed me with a husband who is ready, willing, and able to be my support system—as I am ready to be there for him."

Gina Fahleson Boe went on to record other albums. She continues to give inspiration and hope to others as she shares her remarkable story during her concerts. When Gina interrupts her performance to play part of the tape from her early speech therapy sessions, it gives new meaning to the words of her songs. "This is a song I wrote with Ted Eschliman that summarizes a major lesson I learned about trusting God through that difficult experience," Gina tells her audience. Then her face lights up as she sings an upbeat song with the following chorus:

> . . . I will trust you
> I know you know what's best for me
> I'll trust you
> In times when it's so hard to see your plan
> When it's hard to understand
> I will just be still and trust your will for me.[1]

TOUGH IT OUT

Sometimes it is not easy to put the past behind and trust God for today. Perhaps you are in a situation where a loss cannot be restored to "better than ever," and you don't see light on the horizon. Even in your darkest moments, God can give you the strength to tough it out. And your life may become full and satisfying in spite of your loss. You can become an inspiration to others, as Ron did.

When he was nine years old, Ron Gustafson had already impressed schoolmates and teachers with his athletic ability—which came as no surprise to those in the community. He was the fourth son in a family that excelled in sports. His father, Don, 240 pounds and 6'6", was a former athlete who had an opportunity to play basketball at the university. Ron's older brothers excelled in baseball, football, and basketball during high school and went on to compete at the college level.

Then one fall afternoon, as Ron was helping his father with chores on the family farm, a freak accident occurred. Ron was riding on the right fender of the tractor as his father drove along a gravel road when a bolt on the axle broke and the tire spun off the hub. The tractor lurched and Ron was thrown beneath the hub. His right arm was severed at the neck. The tibia, the largest of the two bones in his right leg, was crushed. Ron's father picked up Ron and ran a quarter of a mile home for help.

Ron was not expected to live. There were long weeks of hospitalization while doctors labored to restore the injured leg. In a series of more than fifteen operations, bone was taken from Ron's hip and grafted into the crushed tibia, muscles were moved to the front along the shin area, and skin was grafted over the wound. "I just knew I had to tough it out," Ron told reporters a year later. "I prayed for strength."

Ron's family pulled together and supported each other. Friends in the community offered prayers and practical help. "Our doctor was wonderful," Ron's mother says. "We were later told by other specialists that if we had had anyone else Ron's leg would have been amputated. One day when Dr. Chleborad came out of surgery he just looked at us and said, 'There was someone greater than me in there today' and walked away. We still don't know exactly what happened."

A year and a half later, a reporter for the *Omaha World-Herald* wrote:

> Prayers were answered. Ronnie lived. And one day he returned to Jerry Mathers's fourth grade class. He came back, Mathers remembers, with a grin on his face and the same competitive fire in his heart.
>
> "Ronnie had left as a leader and nothing had changed," Mathers said. "He was still a leader. The kids looked up to him as one who knew how to act in a time of crisis."
>
> They still do.
>
> When you are 10 or 12, it is difficult to put feelings into words. It is hard to define inspiration. But Jeff Schoch, a 10-year-old classmate, tried: "All the kids admire Ronnie. Watching him makes us want to be better persons, too."
>
> Charley Jessen is 12, a sixth grader. "I guess he taught us how to handle something bad," he said. "Ever since what happened to him, I try to do better with what I have."[2]

As soon as Ron was home, he began to relearn skills and to work on improving the strength in his left arm. He sat on a chair in the garage and played catch with his dad, always working on accuracy. When Ron's condition improved, his dad brought home a bucketful of new baseballs and set up a backstop. Ron would work for hours, throwing them again and again then pausing to retrieve them. Even with a cast on his leg, Ron was back competing in the junior high basketball program.

The school did as Ron's parents asked: "Let him do exactly as the other children. If he fails—so be it. Normal children fail at times. He isn't to have any special treatment or pampering."

At home Ron's older brothers gave him no concessions when shooting hoops. By the time Ron entered high school, his ball-handling skills were outstanding. Ron started on the varsity team as a sophomore, led the team in blocked shots, and was third in rebounds. At the North Dakota University basketball camp, Ron claimed the tenth grade division championship in the one-on-one competition.

During high school Ron continued to provide leadership on the basketball team and won more honors. Off the court Ron related to others with poise and good humor, winning many friends.

Ron went on to make the basketball team at Kearney State College, but he was sidelined with injuries when the knee of his good leg was weakened from overuse. Although he was no longer competing athletically, off the court Ron's winning style remained. He was elected homecoming king at Kearney State, yet when friends called to congratulate him, Ron was more excited about an upcoming opportunity to speak to teenagers through the Fellowship of Christian Athletes.

Ron's speeches have inspired many young athletes to work hard and to put their faith in Jesus. "I don't ask for sympathy from anyone, and no one takes it easy on me. I consider myself an equal," Ron said in a television interview. "I don't set my limitations. I let the Lord set my limitations, and I can do anything that He wants me to do. And I *will* do anything He wants me to do."

Looking back, Ron's mother recalls the constructive steps they took to stay close as a family. "We openly loved each other. And we were sure to *tell* our boys and each other we loved them. It's something we knew, but we felt the boys must hear it. We needed to be sure to hug them and express our love—not just expect them to know it. We took a day at a time and tried to do what was best." For those in the middle of stressful circumstances, she suggests, "When there's work to be done, *do it* and go on—don't chew on it forever! Pull together."

Ron is now happily married and is launching a new company that sells microfiche and computer data systems. Ron's wife summarizes Ron's outlook this way, "Ron basically did the best he could to prove negative-minded people wrong regarding his abilities. He always did his best and pushed himself as he would have had to do regardless of the accident. He just knew to accomplish anything he was going to have to work twice as hard. Goals were very important to Ron and still are in his life."

Family commitment, faith, and determination helped the Gustafson family tough it out during the hardest times. A lot of work went into it. But the bonding and happiness they had together was worth the effort. For those who are currently living through tough times, Ron offers these words of encouragement, "Don't give up on yourself. Turn a setback into a comeback!"

LOVE AS YOU GO

Life is short. There isn't time for endless wondering about what might have been or moping about plans that had to be set aside. You cannot afford to wait until life is running smoothly to improve your relationships. Tragedy and trials can serve to bind your family together. The challenge is to learn how to love as you go.

Arlan and Rita know that Erin will need another open-heart surgery, but they don't talk much about that, as Arlan explains, "We don't get geared up to run the next race until the hurdles are set up. We've learned not to wear ourselves out worrying about what's ahead. We pace ourselves, and enjoy the normal pleasures of family life as they come."

When we share some of the tough times the Schweitz family has gone through during the last ten years or what they may face in the near future, it is easy to give a false impression. Life is not, and has not ever been, all bad.

Rita explains, "We have good memories that outnumber and overshadow the difficult days—like the times we have built snowmen, gone to the zoo, or had water fights on the lawn.

"Our kids grew up asking the same sort of questions most little kids come up with: 'Why does water get dirt wet?' 'If milk comes from cows, does water come from fish?' 'Can Jesus see with His eyes closed?' And the classic: 'I know that babies grow in their mommy's tummy, but what I don't know is how do they get started in there?'"

Rita and Arlan believe that they are a very ordinary family that has learned to enjoy life as it comes. They are determined, like the Gustafsons were, that whatever they face will not tear them apart or destroy the love in the family. Rita admits that they do not perfectly apply the principles in this book, but they have discovered the truth in Emerson's words: "That which we persist in doing becomes easier—not that the nature of the task has changed, but our ability to do has increased."

The Chinese symbol for the word *crisis* stands for both "danger" and "opportunity." It seems fitting in regard to our relationships. A crisis brings pressures, irritations, demands, frustrations, hurts. But it also provides an opportunity to grow closer, to care for one another, and to improve the ways we relate with those we love.

Perhaps those who have felt stranded on the tightrope of stress can best appreciate the comfort provided by a safety net of interdependent relationships. Where does the tightrope lead? If you so choose, it can lead to greater maturity and deeper love for one another. With God's help, we can each begin now, even in less than ideal circumstances, to change ourselves and our relationships for the better. It can be done! You can do it.

Notes

Chapter 4 Don't Look Down

1. William Raspberry quoted in *The Reader's Digest*,

Chapter 6 One Step at a Time

1. Lewis Carroll, *Alice's Adventures in Wonderland* (Secaucus, NJ: Castle Books, 1978), 41.
2. Frank Minirth and Paul Meier, *Happiness Is a Choice: Overcoming Depression* (Grand Rapids, MI: Baker, 1978), 15.

Chapter 7 Held Steady by Faith

1. Nick Stinnett and John DeFrain, *The Secrets of Strong Families* (Boston: Little, Brown, 1985), 100.
2. Sandra P. Aldrich, "Single But Not Alone," *Living Through the Loss of Someone You Love* (Lincoln, NE: Back to the Bible, 1990), 30.
3. Evelyn Boswell, "My Journey of Thanks," *Decision*, June 1991, 6.
4. An adaptation of this story written by Rita Schweitz appears in *Mary in a Martha's World: Quiet Times for Busy Mothers* (Minneapolis, MN: Augsburg Fortress, 1989).

Chapter 8 The Balance Poles

1. John DeFrain, Linda Ernst, Deanne Jakub, Jacque Taylor, *Coping with Sudden Infant Death* (Lexington, MA: Lexington Books, The Free Press, Macmillan, 1991).

2. Carol Travilla, *Caring without Wearing* (Colorado Springs, CO: NavPress, 1990), 42.

Chapter 10 When Emotions Trip You Up

1. Paul Tournier, *A Doctor's Casebook in the Light of the Bible* (New York: Harper & Row, 1960), [as quoted in *Happiness Is a Choice*, Frank Minirth and Paul Meier (Grand Rapids: Baker, 1978), 71–72.]
2. Dr. Robert Hemfelt, Dr. Frank Minirth, and Dr. Paul Meier, *We Are Driven* (Nashville, TN: Thomas Nelson, 1991), 271.
3. Nancy K. Austin, "Race Against Time—and Win," *Working Woman*, Nov. 1990, 48.
4. Shad Helmstetter, *Choices* (New York: Pocket, 1989), 35.
5. Norman Cousins, *Head First* (New York: E.P. Dutton, 1989), 21, 288.
6. Ibid., 73.

Chapter 12 Critical Illness

1. The American Cancer Society, *Facts and Figures 1991.*
2. Elizabeth Berg, "Moments of Ease," *Special Report on Health*, Jan. 1991, 9.
3. Dr. James Dobson, interviewing Philip Yancey for *Where Is God When It Hurts?* "Focus on the Family," 1982, 1986.
4. Philip Yancey, ibid.
5. Libba Bray, "Putting On Make-Up," *Special Report on Health*, Jan. 1991, 10.
6. Tim Hansel, *You Gotta Keep Dancin'* (Elgin, IL: David C. Cook, 1985), [as quoted in "Through the Pain," *World Challenge*, Jan–Feb 1991, 22.]
7. Beth Leuder, "Through the Pain" *World Challenge*, [Jan–Feb] 1991, 22–23.
8. Ibid., 23.
9. Berg, "Moments of Ease," 9.
10. Elisabeth Elliot, *A Path Through Suffering* (Ann Arbor, MI: Servant, 1990), 81, 82.

11. Paul West, "After a Stroke," *Special Report on Health*, Jan. 1991, 10.

Chapter 14 Financial Setbacks

1. Stinnett and DeFrain, *The Secrets of Strong Families*, 137.
2. Ron Blue, *Master Your Money: A Step-by-Step Plan for Financial Freedom* (Nashville, TN: Thomas Nelson, 1986), 19.

Chapter 15 Turning a Setback into a Comeback

1. Gina Fahleson Boe, "I Will Trust You," Copyright 1990 Gina Boe Music, Lincoln, NE. [(402-488-9560)]. All rights reserved. Used by permission.
2. Al Frisbie, "Plucky Lyons Boy 'Toughs It Out,'" *Sunday World-Herald*, March 6, 1977.

Richard Fowler, Ed.D., is a licensed professional counselor with the Texas State Board of Examiners and is the director of clinical services for the Minirth-Meier Clinic of Dallas and Longview, Texas. His doctoral degree is in the field of social psychology.

Dr. Fowler has served as professor at three different colleges in the last eighteen years and has acted as a consultant and a management trainer and seminar leader for a wide variety of corporations.

Co-author of *The Path to Serenity* and the Serenity Meditation™ Series devotion *Day by Day, Love Is a Choice*, Dr. Fowler is a frequent guest on the national radio call-in program, "The Minirth-Meier Clinic," and ACTS television program, "COPE." He represents the clinics nationally, as a speaker and teacher.

Rita Schweitz is a freelance writer and songwriter and a former teacher and coach of junior and senior high students. Author of the book *Mary in Martha's World*, her articles have been published in magazines such as *Moody Monthly*, *Decision*, *Christian Living*, and *Today's Child*.

Rita graduated Phi Beta Kappa from University of Nebraska. She lives with her husband and children in Oakland, Nebraska.

Richard Fowler and Rita Schweitz are available for seminars across the country on maintaining healthy and balanced relationships during tough times. You can reach them by calling the Minirth-Meier Clinics' Speakers' Bureau (214) 669-1733 or by calling Laughter and Joy Bookstore in Oakland, Nebraska, (800) 676-6761.